Nail Your Novel: Why Writers Abandon Books and How You Can Draft, Fix and Finish With Confidence
Roz Morris

Okay, that's the warning stuff over. Now enjoy writing.

A Kindle edition of this book is available from Amazon UK and Amazon.com

www.nailyournovel.com

Nail Your Novel

**Why Writers Abandon Books
and How You
Can Draft, Fix and Finish
with Confidence**

Roz Morris

Also by Roz Morris

My Memories of a Future Life
Available July 2011

Contents

1 Why people start novels and don't finish 19

2 Before you start the manuscript 35

3 The first draft 73

4 Before you rewrite 113

5 The rewrites 134

6 Sending your novel to seek its fortune 156

Introduction

Have you got a novel inside you? Many people say they have. They'll get round to writing it some day – just not now. Or, if now is the perfect time, they're not sure how to go about it.

Maybe you already write. In which case you know there's a lot to worry about. Character, plot, arcs, plot points, tone, narrators, narrative, viewpoint, metaphor, themes, language, imagery, genre, research, pacing. Phew. You'll probably also know that a novel is a holistic organism in which each of those elements sparks off all the others.

How do you hit all those marks AND make a fascinating story?

Most things we do we have a plan for. In most jobs, if we have a task to do, there's a project plan, a schedule, a methodology. But many people start a novel and hope they'll muddle through.

I've been writing novels for years and helping floundering writers find their way. What I notice time and time again is that so many make it very hard for themselves, even experienced authors.

I'm not saying writing a novel is easy. Nor that anyone could do it. But there are ways to make it much harder than it needs to be.

For instance, many writers paint themselves into a corner because they are tackling a problem at the wrong time. They get blocked because the critical parts of their brain are inhibiting their creativity. Or their overactively inventive imagination is stopping them seeing the simple, rational solution. Or they are attempting to spice up a dull story by adding more events, when really they need to find a way to examine the ones they already have.

There are times when you can usefully fret about phrasing, or whether your character saw her boyfriend last week or last night. And there are times when that is a huge waste of energy.

I hate wasting energy. And as a professional I can't afford to. I've developed a method to tackle all the milestones of writing a novel, from initial inspiration to final polish. It's smart and efficient. It draws on techniques from Hollywood scriptwriting, improvisational drama, project management and sports psychology – because experts in those fields have already solved problems that novel-writers come across.

I'm going to tell you the way to nail your novel.

Who am I?

I am a professional writer with more than a dozen finished novels under my belt. I ghost as other people and I write under my own name. Eight of my novels are bestsellers.

I also freelance for a critiquing consultancy. I love stories and storytelling – if you do too, drop in on my website, www.nailyournovel.com – inspiration and creative provocation for writers.

My method will not only help you finish a novel, it makes the whole writing business a lot more creative and fun. A thoroughly planned novel takes less time to write. Even better, it is more likely to succeed in today's market because it will have been properly structured, fixed and polished.

If you've never finished writing a novel before, imagine how you'd feel if you got all the way to the end.

What this book is

This book is a complete project plan for writing a novel. It's a short book because there's no need to make it a long one. And if you're trying to start a novel you don't need yet another thing to do before you can begin. Your time is precious and you need to get going.

Some writing guides make you go through a series of exercises to warm you up before you embark on a 'proper' piece of writing. *Write 200 words every morning on a noun picked at random from the dictionary* – that sort of thing. There's none of that here because I don't believe that's necessary. This is the age of communication. You can all text, email, tweet, blog, comment, review and write letters. You already know how to put your thoughts into prose.

What I will make you do is quite a lot of tasks that aren't writing the actual text of your book. But they will all be work on your novel. But no exercises, no time wasting. From the word go, you are getting on with your novel. This is all work that will shape the finished book.

How to use this book

This is not a book about the detailed mechanics of plot, character etc, although I will give thumbnail notes on the essentials when you need to be thinking especially about them. There are many good books that go into those aspects of writercraft in exhaustive detail, and we all have our own favourites according to the genre we write and the kind of tutoring we relate to.

But this plan can be used no matter what genre you want to write. Whether you're a first-timer or an old timer.

It will help you use stories – and what you learn from other books – to the maximum because you will get the best out of your ideas.

It will also enable you to troubleshoot. Not just logistical problems such as how to get your characters out of a sinking boat, or how to spot if your plotting's a mess.

Writers also need to battle hiccups in their confidence and motivation. I know all the enemies to writing and the destroyers of creativity. I'll help you outsmart them. The bad times when you don't know what to do, or you're fed up with the manuscript. Where your creativity is mired in sludge and your writer's block goes from wall to wall.

All these problems have solutions if you know how to find them.

Start now – right now

You can start work now. The step-by-step process will tell you all you need to do as you go along. Your working day starts with a cup of coffee and this book. You read a bit, then do as it says. When you've completed that task, read a bit more. I'll anticipate when you're likely to get stuck and I'll tell you how to get out of it.

If you've got a novel abandoned in a drawer, you can use this book to resurrect it. Not just that but your enthusiasm, that little flame of belief that got you all excited in the first place.

Whether you're starting from scratch or revisiting a previous attempt, if you follow the steps all the way to the end you'll have a finished, polished novel in your hands.

Index to resources

Need a plain English reminder about plot points? Check out the Thumbnail Notes. Stuck? Creative gears rusted solid? Telling instead of showing? Not in the mood? Try a creative game, a block buster or a rescue remedy.

Thumbnail notes...

Creative games for plotting

Creative games for assessing a draft

Techniques to make your brain show, not tell

Block busters

Tricks to make you do the work properly

Rescue remedies for a sprawling draft

1 Why people start novels but don't finish

Let me tell you a little story. Long ago, I had an idea for a novel. I'd got a set-up and some characters, and a cracking setting based on a place I knew. The creative sap was rising and I couldn't contain myself any longer. I plunged in and started writing. It started so purposefully and I thought I'd just see where it went.

After a couple of weeks I was finding each day more difficult. The characters had headed up several dead ends and I didn't know what to do.

You wouldn't have known the book was so aimless by looking at the beginning. I used to go to a writers' group, and I read out the first 20,000 words over the course of a few weeks. The opening contained the lightning bolt of inspiration – everyone loved it and was intrigued.

Where on earth would it go, they asked. I wished I knew.

But I don't give up easily. I ground out 60,000 words before I had to admit nothing had developed and it wasn't getting any better. I could not squeeze out any more twists, or think of anything else the characters could do. I hated what I'd got them into and couldn't see how to rescue it. Writing it became like torture, a treadmill with no ending.

The five big problems

There are five main reasons why people start writing novels and don't finish them.
- They ground to a halt after the first flush of enthusiasm
- They kept seeing other books they wanted to make it like and kept changing their mind
- They lost confidence
- They had to leave it for a while and then couldn't pick up the thread
- They don't get much time to write

How the method solves these problems

Problem 1: You grind to a halt after the first flush of enthusiasm

Some of us are lucky and can start a manuscript with little planning and keep going until the end. Most of us can't, myself included, and find it all turns ugly.

Most successful writers spend a long time planning before they write a word of the actual text. They don't plunge into the text straight away. In fact, that's the stage they're often reluctant to start, cheerfully referring to all their research and mulling as procrastination. Of course, some take this to ridiculous lengths, but in most cases it's sensible.

Solution You plan where you're going so you won't run out of ideas. I can always move forwards with the novel I'm working on.

I never have a day when I'm sitting there with my mind an endless blank from horizon to horizon like the white wastes of the Arctic.

I do get stuck, but temporarily and on a minute scale – a matter of not knowing how to get from one scene to the next. Sometimes that can be bad enough, like the moment in a Bugs Bunny cartoon where the hero discovers that the small crack across his path is a yawning crevasse that goes all the way down to the bottom of the world. But getting across only takes a short hop.

Problem 2: You keep seeing other books you want it to be like

Often this happens because you hadn't tested your idea strongly enough.

Solution You don't start writing until you're fully committed to your novel and satisfied with the way you want to do it. You know what you want to write and what kind of story you want to tell. You're pleased with it and not so likely to have your confidence dented by reading something else.

Problem 3: You lost confidence

Writers write well when they feel confident and comfortable. But it also helps to know you can finish, and that when you encounter problems you can sort them out. Established writers aren't put off by lapses in inspiration or other bugbears because they know what to do about them. This coping mechanism is often what novice writers lack

Solution This is really the same problem as #2. Planning your book will give you confidence. I'll show you how to devise developments that will excite you, so you will be involved and immersed in the story and want to keep writing all the way to the end.

Problem 4: You had to leave it for a while and couldn't pick up the thread

Real life, with non-made-up people, has a habit of getting in the way of hobbies and routines. And when you come back to your novel, it looks like alien babble.

Worse, you can't remember what you were going to do next. How will you ever get back into it?

It's not only amateurs or beginner writers who have this problem. Working writers have often got several books or projects on the go at once. They'll finish one, then have to start revisions on another they last looked at months before.

Solution Having proper preparation documents helps you get back into the swing of your novel quickly. It's far more efficient than just picking up the manuscript, trying to work out where you'd got to, what your underlying purpose was with everything and what was going to happen next.

So if you need to put your novel aside to get on with something more pressing in the real world, you can easily pick up where you left off.

Problem 5: Don't get much time to write

Solution We all have greater and lesser amounts of spare time. You have to see writing as a regular activity in your life; a routine like your gym sessions or studying for professional exams. Writing must be first a resolution and then a habit. It is not something to dip into when you've got the time.

The difficulty many novice writers have is that they are stopping themselves committing to writing. It is solitary; an indulgent and fantasy world that excludes real people. A frivolous hobby, learned haphazardly by tinkering. It's never going to amount to anything. They don't tell anyone else they do it and they fear that real writers would unmask them and run away cackling.

If that's you, you have to push those negative thoughts aside. We were all beginners once, but those of us who succeeded decided writing was important and prioritised it as a thing we did routinely.

The good news is that you can do a lot of valuable work on your novel without any kind of pen or writing instrument. On the bus, on the tube, walking to the station. With your hands on a steering wheel, a set of weights, a carving knife and an onion. This is called thinking time and it's every bit as valuable as typing or scribbling. Then, when you get the opportunity to lock yourself away with a pen or a PC, you'll be focussed, you'll have something to write and you'll be able to make the most productive use of your time.

Other realities of writing life

1 Writer's block

Whole books and websites are written about writer's block. It's described in a number of ways, which mainly come down to lack of ideas, lack of enthusiasm. And those all boil down to confidence or a lack of it. You believe you haven't got anything good to write, or anything to write at all. And so you stop.

That's the big mistake. Giving up. Writing is not just about doing it when you feel the muse is flowing. It's about doing it, period. If you're the kind of person who believes that block will stop you, you're the type to get it.

Of course, writing is not easy. Or maybe I should say, writing well is not easy. Even successful authors don't find it easy.

Working writers know that writing is a craft and a job. They don't waste hours of hard-earned writing time wondering what to do. So says Henry Miller: 'when you can't create, work'. And Agatha Christie: 'I assumed the burden of a profession, which is to write even when you don't want to, don't much like what you are writing and aren't writing particularly well'.

To finish a novel you need persistence and stamina. And purpose. With my method, you won't start writing anything until you are properly prepared. And so you will always have something to write.

2 Writing is rewriting...

You will notice that my system involves going over aspects of your novel again and again. Sometimes tearing it apart – again and again.

The vast majority of the words you write, you will have to rewrite, edit, cut, remove, put back again, have a think and rejig yet again.

That might look very inefficient, not to mention a mite boring. But writing novels is a process of repeating and refining.

All writers have to rewrite their novels. Several times. It's simply part of the process. Novice writers don't realise that this is normal.

There are writers who claim to write only one draft and get it perfect – but they will have done all the editing in their head first of all. Personally, I don't feel comfortable planning in my head. I fear I'll forget things, so I write everything down.

Generally a novel is written millimetre by millimetre, by planning, writing, rewriting – and usually rewriting again.

It can be gruelling. Philip Roth says: 'Over the years what you develop is a tolerance for your own crudeness. Stay with your crap and it will get better, and come back every day and keep going'.

Just as all writers were beginners once, so were all novels. They all went through rough stages, even the ones by our most hallowed masters. But these are the stages where novices might easily lose hope and give up.

2.1 Writing is not always writing
Writing a novel will present you with an unbelievable number of problems to solve, a thousand ways of presenting a scene or drawing a character. They all require different ways of thinking – logical left brain, dreamy right brain. And, at times, various combinations of the two.

A lot of these problems are not best solved by sitting at the manuscript with a red pen, or doing the keyboard equivalent. There are much smarter ways to work them out. In fact, a lot of them are not a lot like work and more like playing games.

FAQs

1 Won't a 'system' kill creativity?

Non-writers are surprised when I explain I have a system for writing, with design and testing stages like building a bridge. They remark that this surely must stultify creativity. That depends on how you go about it.

Beginners tend to think that the only creative part is when you are writing the textfiles that will eventually be the book. But there are ways to make the whole process intensely creative, from initial brainstorming to final editing.

A lot of it involves making notes. There are ways to make notes that will squash your creativity flat. Or to end up with thousands of them in a disorganised mess that's next to useless. But there are ways to write your notes that are very useful indeed.

2 And spontaneity?

It takes a while to write a novel of 100,000 words or thereabouts. We're talking months, maybe years. After that amount of time questions of spontaneity seem a bit laughable.

3 How can a system help you write a much better book?
I remember reading a book about tuning pianos, which said it is perfectly possible to tune a piano just by ear, without the help of tuning forks, but if you do you will probably end up with all the notes sounding the same. If I wrote a novel without my bag of tools, I'd get a great start but no structure, pace, crescendos, diminuendos, developments, pay-offs, and no satisfactory closure. Or probably no closure at all. Everything would remain stuck at the start.

That's just me; beginnings are my inspiration. For other writers, it's all one character, or a plotline. But if you can develop all your story elements and make them work together, you'll have a much better novel.

4 Why all the steps?
You'll see that quite a lot of the time you will be going over things again and again. Because you can't get it all right first time.

In the world of work, everyone knows that if you have to accomplish a big task, you split it into small ones. Most writers who give up are trying to do the wrong thing at the wrong time. Or trying to do too much. No wonder they can't cope. Efficient writers know what to do at each stage and how to make it count.

Imagine you were building a house. You need to get architects' plans, buy the materials, get the foundations laid, the walls up, stick the electrics and plumbing in. Finally, you decorate. It's far easier to do all the big stuff like designing the foundations in one fell swoop, when you're in a foundations frame of mind. If you had to think about the position of the spotlights at the same time your brain would overload and you'd do neither well.

And so it is with a novel. The brain can handle certain types of thinking at some stages, and other types at other stages.

In particular, sweating over details at the wrong time can make you feel like you have an endless, unfinishable task.

In this book I will tell you what to focus on and when – and what to ignore until later. Efficient writers are never reading their work aimlessly and tweaking a sentence here and there. I give you mechanisms that allow you to pull back and test if your novel works, assess what adjustments to make, and then zoom back in and sort them out.

This principle of leaving certain problems until later in the process takes the pressure off and allows you to make full use of your creative faculties without having to get everything perfect first time. It's effective and very liberating.

Your personality type

What stage of writing you find most difficult depends on your temperament. For me, it's the first draft. I'm a perfectionist and I notice details all the time, so I hate writing anything that is going to be tidied up later. I spend so much time in a first draft feeling it isn't going well. All I notice is how rough it is; I don't see the good ideas that are flowing.

It doesn't help that I was an editor for years, cleaning up other people's prose, so a clumsy sentence or a dull scene nags away like a foot kicking my chair. Of course I love the sense of immersion when a scene goes well and takes me by surprise, but that inner critic ruins it for me, like a sour, criticising aunt.

You may have heard of the Belbin test, which is a way to measure what kind of role you are suited to in a team. In Belbin terms, I'm a 'completer-finisher' and roughness worries me. Belbin 'shapers', who come up with ideas but lose the impetus to see them through to the end, have different problems.

There are other ways to measure your brain's tendencies, according to whether you're emotional or logical, instinctive or judgemental, and so on. Belbin also talks about 'plants', who stimulate other people to have ideas. You could analyse it all to death but with novel-writing it all comes down to one thing.

How to tame your inner critic.

We all need our inner critic. It's what makes us raise our game and improve what we do. We certainly need it if we're trying to write a good novel. But if your inner critic threatens to sabotage your book, at whatever stage, you need to tell it to pipe down. That's what my games are designed to do.

With my system you give your inner critic specific tasks. Completer-finishers can tell it when to shut up and when it's welcome to help them out. If your inner critic isn't too boisterous and noisy, you might be able to get on with the first draft sooner. (Although you may find it useful to leave some of the tasks until later, as you will at some stage have to assess the structure of your novel.) Shapers and plants can use the creative games to keep their interest fresh in the later stages and give themselves new problems to solve.

Tailor the system to your needs

Depending on how fully formed your idea is, you might not need to go through every task. What I have written is a plan starting from a blank piece of paper with just a couple of ideas for where you want to go.

That's usually what professionals start with, but not all novels are going to need so much development. If you've been incubating an idea for some time you might already have a rough idea of the beginning, middle and end, so you won't have to sweat over those.

How long should you spend on each task?

That's entirely up to you. You might be using a setting or writing about a subject that you know from personal experience, so research will be negligible.

But if you are starting from scratch don't underestimate how much preparation a novel might take.

The children's novelist Alan Garner used to spend an entire year researching for one of his books. In his case, not much of it was factual – he'd read mythology, other novels, books about the landscape he was going to use. After roughly 365 days of allowing his subconscious to shuffle and sort what he was reading, he'd suddenly think of a last line. Yes the last line, not the first. And then he knew he was ready to start writing.

Ian Fleming, on the other hand, used to write a first draft and then do the research. Another draft and he was done. That certainly looks more streamlined than my system – but he already had a lot of his work done. He had a strong template to follow so he knew what ingredients he needed – exotic locations, glamour and danger, girls and villains with dashing names and a thrilling finale. He also knew who his main character was. The research was icing on the cake.

And then there's the actual writing. Isabel Allende always writes the first line on 8 January, because it was the date she started both her first and her second novels. 'I have not dared change that auspicious date, partly out of superstition and also for reasons of discipline.' Read her memoir *Paula* and it's clear she spends many months incubating the ideas, but the first word does not hit the page until the second week of January.

Jeffrey Archer never felt he'd finished unless he'd done a magic 12 revisions.

You might like to start on a ritual date or use a certain pen. These all help make you feel comfortable, but true confidence comes from sound preparation.

If you're already sure of many of your elements you can skip some of the stages. But the stages are all tasks that go into making a good, working novel. Some people like to plan in their head and hardly write anything down. That's still planning.

Even if you largely know where you're going you still might find it useful to play some of the creative games. They're designed to unlock potential you never knew your story had. And to spot the holes you didn't know were there.

Got an abandoned manuscript you want to finish?

If you've got a manuscript sleeping somewhere, completed or otherwise, you can use some of the exercises to assess it.

- For an unfinished draft, try Task 3 on p48.
- If you've got enough material already but you suspect you could use it better or that there are big holes in the plot, go to Task 4, page 52. I'm certainly going to use it to give that 60,000-word meandering monster a work-out.
- Use Task 4 for finished drafts too, if you suspect you may want to beef up the plot or do heavy restructuring.

- If you're fairly happy with the plot and structure, but want to examine the manuscript in more detail, try Task 8, on p117.

One final point

When I say take a break it's important to. Or you'll never be able to self-edit. You can get exhausted with looking at the same characters again and again, and bored with your story. There will be times when you wish it was all over. Just as often, hopefully, there will be times when you're very excited about all you've done.

You're not going to get your novel perfect all in one go and there are several phases where you will have to decide, objectively, what works and what doesn't. This comes entirely down to your critical judgement. You must be able to look at your manuscript as if for the first time.

Stephen King puts his first drafts away for a minimum of six weeks before he even thinks about looking at them again. In that time, he writes other things, goes fishing, stops thinking about the niggling problems in the book and just forgets about it.

So when you take a break, get the book out of your hair and out of your head.

Right. Let's get on with it.

2 Before you start the manuscript

What are you trying to get right at this stage?

You're going to liberate your creativity. Answer the big questions about your book. By the end of this stage you will have a detailed story plan. You'll know who your characters are. What kind of story you're writing. What that story is, where it starts and where it finishes. What the settings are. The era. You'll have researched your settings and anything else you need.

You may have an inkling about your themes, although these sometimes change when you look at a completed draft. You will be well on the way to getting the most out of your themes, characters and story.

You'll be prepared to start writing. The preparation you have done will make the writing go a lot faster. You are less likely to get blocked and more likely to sail through to the end.

What are you ignoring for now?
Creating detailed scenes – unless inspiration strikes and you jot it down in a notepad. In this task you will not be writing one word of the actual manuscript.

Task 1 Shaping your inspiration

All my books start with a few ideas flung together. An inspiration for a situation someone might be in, the kind of person that might happen to, a setting that seems potent with mischief or power. I don't have to tell you what initial inspiration is like – that's why you're here.

I have a folder on my computer in which I have several textfiles which are collections of ideas for future novels. It may seem rather anal retentive to mention this. But there's an important point. Not all the great ideas you have will sit happily together in one novel. If you try to make them, you might end up with a sprawling mess. Good novels are focused, they don't have things that are irrelevant. If you get used to that idea from the start, it's easier to write a better novel.

It's also a useful discipline for editing. Later on you'll have to take out things that don't fit, and some of them will be things you like.

(You may have heard authorly types intoning the phrase 'kill your darlings'. Indeed I shall do it to you later. That's what it means – getting rid of the phrases, ideas or characters that are in there only because you like them and not because they fit.)

Many of the darlings you kill would probably be perfectly good in some other book you write. It pays to develop the habit of taking ideas out and keeping them for another day.

Even if you're embarking on your first novel ever, do this. Most people who have the yen to write one novel have the temperament to keep thinking of ideas for other ones.

Task 2 Starting this specific novel

Write down your inspirations and ideas for your novel. You might not get very much all in one go, so keep coming back and adding to it. I write down ideas for developments, events, characters and twists as they occur to me.

At this stage don't worry about the order of events, just the ingredients you want to use. This also gives you a feel for the world of the book, makes it start to seem real.

Keep going until you know:
- who the hero is, who might oppose them
- what these people are trying to do
- what the setting is – both geographically and socially
- what might complicate the drama (a murder, a disappearance, a divorce, an exploding spaceship)
- why that will be a long story not a short one
- what kicks off the situation
- where it will end
- what the genre is

sense of purpose and the forces that will oppose the hero.

Any plot needs obstacles, goals and complications. They may be physical or psychological, but they still have to be there. Plots will seem lifeless without them and a story will have nowhere to go. The forces that oppose the hero should be other characters, if at all possible (a particular detective or sheriff, rather than 'the law' as an anonymous set of rules).

Also check out your central characters. Make sure you are intending them to DO things, rather than agonise while trouble happens to them. Make them active, not passive. No one wants to read about people who sit around thinking 'this is hard for me because I'm sensitive'. Although readers can relate to sensitivity, and such people are nice to have as your friends in real life, they are not interesting to read about for very long.

The people who ARE interesting to read about are the ones who will respond to a challenge, who will try to do something to change their lives, or to right a wrong. They're not the ones who avoid a fight or who wait and see if everything gets better. And you need more than one person like that – preferably the hero and the person who is opposing them.

So many novels, or would-be novels, fail because the main characters are dull and won't do anything. If you suspect there's anything dull about your story, see if it's the characters.

Thumbnail notes... Characters and trouble – conflict

All good fiction comes down to characters, no matter what the genre. Thrillers need active characters, but so does literary fiction. Jane Austen's heroines were not wimps. They try to change things. The main character could even be someone who had previously waited to see if things would get better, but now, in these circumstances, they will finally have to DO something.

'Trouble' need not be a murder or a stalker. It could be the new stepfather to your hero's grandchildren, or their provocatively fanciable co-star in a romantic film. It could be a job they realise they can no longer stand. It is whatever life event kicks the hero in a way they just can't ignore.

The general 'trouble' or 'conflict' elements are the hero versus:
- Themselves
- Society
- The environment or nature (eg *The Day of the Triffids*)
- Other characters, who are competing for the same thing as the hero, or want to do something that might spoil the hero's happiness in some way, or stop the hero getting what they want

Thumbnail notes... **Being genre aware**
If you are writing in a well established genre, you need to be aware of its conventions. Readers have clear expectations of genres.

For instance, romantic comedy or chick-lit usually ends in some kind of 'chase-to-the-airport' sequence where all is nearly lost. This may be a dash to stop the loved one getting on a plane, but it doesn't have to be so literal or madcap. But what you must have is a do-or-die situation where the hero or heroine has to stop their love leaving for ever.

If your novel is going to be a romcom or chick-lit, you'll have to create a situation that can naturally culminate in that or in something that will fulfil the same function. If you don't, the book will not have a climax. So it needs to be in your plan from the earliest stage.

What's your inner critic doing at the moment?

It's making sure you have good answers to those questions. This list may be finished quite quickly, in which case you're ready for the next stage. But if you're struggling, here's what to do.

Problem: Filling the blanks

You probably have some of the elements you need. It might be a fascinating situation (a woman falls in love with her priest), a world you want to write about (the circus), some characters you want to play with (three executives on an outward bound course).

Solution 1: Plot thickeners

The 19th-century French writer Georges Polti described 36 situations found in most stories. See what happens if you stir one – or more than one – into your fledgling story.

- Abduction
- Adultery
- All sacrificed for passion
- Ambition
- An enemy loved
- Conflict with a god
- Crime of love
- Crime pursued by vengeance
- Daring enterprise
- Deliverance

- Disaster
- Discovery of the dishonour of a loved one
- Enmity of a kinsmen
- Erroneous judgement
- Falling prey to cruel misfortune
- Fatal imprudence
- Involuntary crimes of love
- Loss of a loved one
- Madness
- Mistaken jealousy
- Murderous adultery
- Necessity of sacrificing loved ones
- Obstacles
- Obtaining
- Pursuit
- Recovery of a lost one
- Remorse
- Revolt
- Rivalry of kinsmen
- Rivalry of supreme and inferior
- Self-sacrificing for an ideal
- Self-sacrificing for a kindred
- Slaying of a kinsmen unrecognized
- Supplication
- The Enigma
- Vengeance taken for kindred upon kindred.

There may only be 36 items on this list but you only need a few in a story. Plus there are no limits to how you combine them or what you can do with them.

Some suggest certain types of character – but see what happens if you take the less obvious option.

- Put the most inhibited person you could imagine in a situation of 'crime of love' or 'crime pursued by vengeance' – there's a story that would have a long way to go.
- Throw in something socially unacceptable such as a big age gap (*Lolita*) or possible incest (*Wuthering Heights*).
- Turn something on its head. *Woman falls in love with her priest* is not nearly as interesting as *Priest falls in love with woman he takes confession from*.
- Or add something really offbeat and make one of the characters a mermaid (*Splash*).

Solution 2: Inspiration from your reading

Read a few novels that are similar to your idea. Also check out similar ideas in film, theatre and TV. Not to copy what they did, heaven forbid. You are reading to find out how other authors have handled themes, situations and settings like yours – and to decide whether you will do something similar (not too similar, please) or different.

The chances are if you've had a good idea someone has already done something similar. You need to make sure you don't repeat it – but usually there's plenty of scope for a new interpretation.

This research process will seed possible ideas for things that could happen. Ask your inner critic to look particularly for ways in which your treatment of the idea could be more interesting, more unusual than what has been done before. Research doesn't have to be factual. It's anything that will get your creative juices flowing.

Solution 3: The 'wish-not' list

Another exercise that is very important is to decide what you do NOT want the book to be. I call this the 'wish-not' list. Here's where you realise you've actually got a lot further with planning your novel than you think.

Your inner critic can really help you out here. You have probably started a wish-not list subconsciously. There may be a romance but you don't want it centre stage. There may be a politician but you don't want to write about politics. These are creative decisions, and they're just as important as the positive ones of who, what and why.

Make your wish-not list and then write down what those decisions might mean. You want a murder, but if the story isn't to find who did it, what other kinds of story could the murder kick off? Write those down and see what appeals.

If you reject something, ask yourself why. Is it because you've never been there or done the thing, or you don't know anyone who has? Is it something you think you could find out about with enough authenticity to write? You don't have to write what you know – you only have to write what you can GET to know. The chances are, if you're interested in a subject, a place or an era, you can find out enough to convince a reader.

Writers do this all the time. Jilly Cooper never played in a professional orchestra although she wrote several novels about it. Lindsey Davis and Robert Graves never lived in ancient Rome. If you should stick only to what you know, we should worry about the thousands of authors who write about murder.

If you're interested in writing about something, don't let a lack of personal experience inhibit you. Do a bit of preliminary research. See if you like the idea of finding out more about a setting, a subject or an activity and what it might add to your novel.

Look at the basic template list. Use them to play with possibilities and, of course, to reject them. And remember that what you reject is as significant as what you decide to use. A murder needn't become a whodunit; it could become *Crime and Punishment* or *The Secret History*.

By starting with a wish-not list, you end up with a wish list.

Solution 4: Get random

Hopefully you've now got more boxes ticked. Look at the ones you've got left. Try throwing something random into the mix. If you're struggling to establish a setting, grab a guidebook for a European city and decide if that will do. If not, write down the reasons why (too small, no drug scene etc). Now you're making some decisions about what you need – and you can find the city that is right. Or decide you should set all the action on a ranch in Wyoming instead.

A word of warning about reading and research at this stage. It shouldn't be detailed until you're absolutely sure you're going to need it. At the moment your story is broad brushstrokes. You are auditioning settings and subjects for story potential, not buying costumes for them too.

If you decide one of your settings might be Geneva, and you've never been there, don't go and find out all the tiny details right now, there is time for that later. Test first if Geneva is right. All sorts of things might change your mind – the local festivals, the countryside, whether it has an old and creepy subway system. You might decide you'd have more potential in Cleethorpes – so you don't want to have wasted a lot of time finding streetmaps of Geneva, buying guidebooks – or even trying to persuade your loved ones to accompany you on a city break there.

Keep it rough

Eventually you'll join the dots and you'll have a rough plan for how the story will go and who is involved in it. Note that you are writing summaries at this stage.

If specific scenes or even dialogue exchanges occur to you, jot them down in a separate scrapbook file. You certainly want to keep them, but for now you want to concentrate on the big picture.

Also, bear in mind that none of this is set in stone yet. You may not be totally happy about all the decisions in your story plan. That is fine. When you do detailed research and plotting you can change them. Don't, though, leave them blank. If you have something, it is much easier to change it. If you have a big hole, it's much harder and you're more likely to get stuck.

Brainstorming and inspiration

This brainstorming approach may seem to be the antithesis of inspiration. But students of creative writing are taught early on that inspiration comes from graft, not from God. You take an idea and you start working with it.

Other dos and don'ts

- Every time you have a summary document you are happy with, keep a copy. Don't delete them. Much, much later you might have to write a synopsis, especially if you hope to present your book to agents and publishers. Most writers go through agonies trying to distil their 100,000-word novel into two sides of A4. It's much easier to start with a summary document, however inaccurate, because you've already got the shape of the story there.

- Don't worry too much about whether your elements make sense or if you have enough material. You will put that to the test in the next stage.
- As you firm up your ideas, start building a library for your book. Once I'm taking a book to that stage I give it its own shelf in my study and a research folder on my computer, which is all rather satisfying. At last the book is becoming real. My main shopping tools are Amazon, obviously, browsing by subject tags and reader recommendations, and also www.librarything.com.

What you now have

You now have a story plan. If you need to do focussed research, read on. But even if you are writing from your own experiences you might find it beneficial to do some of the steps as they'll help you create a better story. Otherwise, skip to the next stage.

Task 3 Focussed research

This is an important part of the work. Take the time you need. Don't feel you have to get it out of the way in favour of getting on with the 'proper' business of writing.

You know your characters, roughly what they're trying to do, the kinds of activities they might be involved in (the advertising industry, deep-sea diving). Here's where you do an awful lot of reading. Googling. Watching DVDs. Finding experts and chatting to them. Making notes.

Yes, you know that. But what you do with those notes is important.

Don't make lists. For one thing, you can never find what you want. More importantly, lists tie you down to having events happen in a certain order, and this is not the time for you to be deciding that. (Unless your research is some kind of procedure with step-by-step stages, such as how to take an appendix out in a jungle. In which case, put it on a separate file to consult later. In story terms it would be distilled into one line anyway – *Kurt takes out Jessica's appendix in the jungle*.)

This is what I do with my notes.

The hat game

I get a box or a tin and I make each note on a separate piece of paper and throw it in the box. It's a version of the game Who's in the hat, and it would be very cool to use a topper. (However I don't have one, so instead I use an old presentation box some pretty plates came in.)

These ideas may be anything, big or small. A major plot twist; a type of character; the smell of gasoline at a car smash. A chase through the Paris Metro on rollerskates. A treehouse in the Serengeti for a romantic scene – or, more surprising, a break-up.

Research might throw up all sorts of interesting situations. For instance, I was commissioned to write a novel about people selling kidneys in India. Reading about the poverty in the villages inspired the start of the story – a young girl decides to sell her kidney to get her family out of debt. Of course, once she's in the clutches of the butchers, she changes her mind, poor love. Meanwhile her family are desperate to get her back.

Anything I come across with story potential, I scribble down and chuck in the box. I don't worry too much about whether the idea duplicates what is already in there – that's inevitable when you're reading around a subject. Later when I go through the box I'll choose the most suitable one. This also means that if you find a better way to do something, don't rummage to find the original bit of paper. Just scribble it down and toss it in.

As the book begins to inhabit your mind more, you'll have ideas while you're out and about and doing other things. Keep a notepad with you, jot them down and when you get back, throw them in the box.

If the idea requires reference to a book, put a reference on the note so you know where to find the exact details when you do the writing. I also put markers in the actual books, thin slivers of Post-its, of things I might want to use, labelled with *Calcutta at sunset*, *What frostbite feels like*. If I rely on the book indices I'll never find them. By the time I've finished with a book it's got a cowboy fringe of yellow and pink tabs.

This stage doesn't necessarily have to take very long. With some novels I've written, all I've done is read a couple of books and magazine articles, made hardly any notes and I'm ready to move on. But if you need to do a lot more conceptualising or fact-finding, this is the way to do it and make it productive.

What's your inner critic doing?

Browsing. It's great fun, the next best thing to shopping. I know writers who never want this phase to end. The plan you made in Task 2 dictates what you need to find out about. This stage is about brainstorming the what-ifs.

Dos and don'ts

- Don't judge whether something is good, bad or repeats what you've already got. Put it in the box and decide later.
- Do look at your plan to make sure you've covered all the points thoroughly
- Don't be worried if you still haven't solved some problems – there are a few more creative games we can play, and some ideas just solve themselves after you sleep on them. Or, in my case, when I'm doing something where picking up a pen would risk life and limb, such as driving at 70mph on a motorway.

Task 4 A structural survey for your story

A lot of people go to the synopsis phase immediately. But if you're still not ready to commit to an order of events, do this. I call it the cards game.

This is where you make your wish-list and your research into a robust plot. You work out what events you want in the novel and how to make them happen.

The cards game also ensures you have set up plot developments suitably. If someone's going to be felled by peanut allergy, you need to have planted the seeds for that event early on in the story. And, by the same token, the cards game helps you make sure that if you set up an important peanut allergy, it has consequences. The cards game tells you if your story is strong enough and whether there are crucial pieces missing.

Even if you are fairly sure about your order of events, you still might find this exercise useful. An event can mean a whole lot of different things in a story, depending on whether you put it at the beginning, in the middle or at the end. Again, if you write a list too soon it's much harder to change fundamentals like this.

Is the novel based on your own experiences?

If your novel is based on your own experiences this gives you a head start in some ways. You have the plot, the characters, the beginning, middle and end. But novels based on real life often have problems of their own which are difficult to see from the manuscript. Several experiences might amount to the same thing dramatically, structurally or emotionally and make for repetitive reading unless they are condensed. There might be gaps of logic that you need to explain. The cards game can help you use your material in the most effective way.

Cards or spreadsheets

I use index cards or Post-Its for this, and spread them out on the dining table or the lounge rug. But if you share your home with a frolicking dog or rumbustious toddler you might prefer the more protectable environment of spreadsheets.

Take your stack of cards and a marker pen, and sift through all those little bits of paper, writing each event or development on a card.

It's important that you use a big marker pen and small cards. That way, you can only fit a few words on the card – which focuses the mind wonderfully.

Your scrap of paper might have said *Jenny crashes the car she borrowed from her daughter and when she looks in the glove compartment for the breakdown number she finds her lost wallet and realises her daughter stole it from her*.

For the cards I would translate this into *Jenny crashes car, finds wallet.* It's clear then that I need to set it up with another card, *Jenny loses wallet.* That's two events already.

This summarising allows you to see at a glance if logical elements are missing, or if you've got two ideas that amount to the same thing.

It might become obvious there is more you should do with Jenny's discovery because nothing develops from it. You could write *Jenny confronts her daughter.* Or you might write *Jenny searches her daughter's bedroom and finds an expensive watch.* If the latter, you might need some other mysterious behaviour from Jenny's daughter earlier on, so you could think of a few things (*money goes missing, teachers report that school work is suffering*).

Perhaps there could also be a *Jenny sends her daughter for psychotherapy* – after all, she'll have to do something positive about it.

Don't worry too much about how these things will happen if you haven't thought about them before. You'll do that in later stages. In effect this is another of those lovely wish-lists.

Also don't worry about upsetting your plans. If you suddenly think Jenny should hire a private detective, don't squash it because you don't know what it will do to the story.

The cards allow you to play 'what if'. Put it in and see if you like the consequences that follow, the way it will push the story. Details are for later.

Later in the box you might find a scrap of paper that said a diamond necklace would be important in the denouement. You might rewrite the two Jenny cards, substituting necklace for wallet.

No, wait a moment. STOP. I don't like this Jenny stuff. Confronting daughters is all too domestic for this story, it's not the tone I want. And it's rather predictable.

How about if Jenny didn't have a thieving daughter, but a thieving flatmate? Hmm. I like it, that could cause far more trouble. It's far more the kind of story I could write. The relationship with a flatmate might be far more precarious and strange.

How do the Jenny cards work with that? She can borrow the flatmate's car, that will still work. She can confront her. She can certainly search the bedroom – in fact I think I'll swap those two events around so she searches the bedroom first.

What could she find? What about a mysterious phone number? And we need some warnings of trouble – *money goes missing, flatmate comes in with inexplicable injuries*

I like the way that's starting to sizzle. Flatmate it is.

Don't be afraid to experiment. And by using the cards you can check the consequences of your experiments at a glance.

Thumbnail notes... Sub-plots

You generally need more than one story thread: a sub plot as well as a main plot. The sub-plot should come in quite early and may not initially look very related to the main plot, except perhaps in theme. It may even be that you have two plot strands of equal importance and twizzle them together. But in the climax the two must seem intimately related.

Sub-plot checklist

* Make main plot and sub-plot connect with each other as much as possible, even if only thematically
* Try to increase the connections as the novel progresses so that it feels as if the main and sub-plot belong together (and are not two separate novels!)
* Design the crescendos of the sub-plot so that they complement the crescendos of the main plot

Weaving plots and sub-plots can be a major headache. But with the cards you develop all your strands in exactly the same way as you would the main plot – with a starter incident, complications and consequences and an ending.

You might find it helpful to write them in a different colour of marker so that when you slot them into the main story you can see at a glance when you have opportunities to knit them together. And what the effects of doing that will be.

You can have more than one sub-plot, of course. But beware of making your story too cluttered. Make sure you can tie it all together and that your novel will be a coherent whole.

Thumbnail notes... keeping your plot focussed

Some novel plots get big and sprawling and unmanageable because they have too many elements. For a slick plot, focus is essential. I quote scriptwriting guru Lew Hunter: 'In life, one thing happens after another. In drama, one thing happens *because* of another.'

Smart plots draw together threads of things that are already there. The cards game allows you to play with this, and to see at a glance what you could re-use. This is why you must explore the consequences of events you create.

Look at what you've already got in the story. See if you can bring it back in in some form later on. For instance, the phone number Jenny found could come up again and Jenny could follow the lead to see where it goes.

Every time you're tempted to invent new things, see if you can bring back an old one.

Thumbnail notes... reincorporation and plotting

If you've flirted with drama in any form you've probably come across improvisation games. If not you've probably heard of the TV show *Whose Line Is It Anyway*.

Improv games, also known as theatre sports, are exercises in making scenes up on the spot. They're great for making you think of interesting things if you're stuck. Focussing on the rules of the game stops you worrying so much about exactly what you are inventing and lets it flow more. In short, it beckons inspiration to descend.

Here's a game about making up stories. You're given a random list of elements and told to tell a tale with them. A fishing rod, a glowing light, a monk, a fox, and a derelict house. The temptation is to jam them all in quickly, so you've done what you're supposed to. You might say 'there was a monk and he was fishing outside an old house. A fox trotted past and was frightened away by a glowing light.'

It's clear that's not much of a story. You will then wonder what all those characters are going to do for the rest of the story, panic, and invent even more. Pretty soon you can't keep it all in your head. The ideas are like a bagful of gerbils running in all directions and scooting into the distance. Rather than try to put the five key elements together to make some sort of sense, however absurd, you keep adding more.

Experienced storytellers drop those crucial ingredients in all the way along. One will lead to another, or be the solution to a story problem or the way to save the day.

The monk might be fishing with the rod at the beginning, but the fish are being scared away by strange unearthly screams from the derelict house behind him. He goes to investigate. The noise is truly terrifying so he says some prayers. A glowing light appears and he follows it into a room. There's a hole in the floor and when he goes to it he sees a vixen and fox cubs who have fallen into the hole and are making the racket. So the monk lowers his fishing basket through the hole with a fishing rod, pulls them to safety. Then he goes back to his position on the river bank and the fish start biting.

Okay, the story is hardly going to be snapped up by Pixar, but it was made up on the spot. But the crucial point is, I hardly had to add anything new. I reincorporated the fishing rod (and other related equipment he might have) and his profession as a monk (prayers and the glowing light).

Reincorporation is giving a satisfying payoff, using elements you got the reader interested in early on. It's rewarding them for paying attention to your intrigue. After all, intrigue and mystery are only interesting because you're wondering what the answer is. If you keep adding more and more new things, and never developing the ones you've already got, the reader will get annoyed.

When you don't know what to do, or you think you're inventing too much, lay your key elements out and see if there's something you can reincorporate.

I like improv games for freeing up creativity. If you do too, I've got more in the next section, the first draft. Check out p95.

Thumbnail notes... **letting character drive the plotting process**

The cards game necessarily focuses on events and it may look as if it leaves no room for character and motivations.

Actually the opposite is true. By this stage I usually have a rough idea of who the people are, what their worries and agendas are and what pressures are on them. The cards game, where I start deciding the things they will do, helps focus them more.

For instance, Jenny might be the kind of woman to take her thieving flatmate to the pub to discuss it. Or she might try to get someone else to solve the problem.

She might blackmail the flatmate. She might think she deserved it – a very different spin. What Jenny does in this difficult situation is entirely dictated by her unique character.

The cards game works for any type of story, because a story is always about something changing. That applies whether you're writing a twisty thriller or a sensitive study of a relationship.

When to stop

How do you know when you've got enough cards? A novel has to be quite a journey. You usually need several acts, like acts in a play, that come together in a climax.

Usually films are built in three acts – one building from the next, causing increasing amounts of trouble and boiling up to a crescendo. Novels are more fluid of course – you can have fewer than three or more (particularly if it's something like a family saga where you might span many generations). But start off aiming for three and you should have enough substance. The right number will emerge naturally.

Bold strokes, please

You'll notice that at this stage the story is in bold strokes. This is so that you can step back and see the story as scenes, not details. That's why you use a big fat marker pen and small cards, because you can't fit much into that space. It forces you to think big. You start with a cluster of locations in disconnected towns and build a route map to get through all the events and to the end.

What's your inner critic doing?

Looking for flaws, lapses of logic, gaps in the pattern. Identifying a need for a development or scene. Making sure there are enough interesting threads and that the main plot hooks into the sub plot or plots.

What's it not doing?

Worrying about how these scenes will go, or telling you you don't have the knowledge to write them. If you need to know about sending hitmen to sort out errant flatmates it's always possible to find out.

Deciding the order

As you go, spread the cards out over a big table or the floor in a rough order. Don't just accept that order, swap them around. What if Jenny's discovery is right at the beginning? That throws a shadow over all the subsequent events. What if it's at the end as a twist – the epilogue that throws an intriguing spin on everything? In the middle?

You can also try variations – Jenny doesn't have a thieving flatmate, she IS the thieving flatmate. It doesn't take long to scribble a couple of new cards, slot them in and see if you like the result. Depending on where you put it, this event could be anything.

The cards method gets the best out of your story potential and liberates your thinking.

Depending on how complex the story is, you might play with this stage for a few days or even a few weeks. With some novels I find there's a lot of mind-changing, shuffling and trying things out. That's okay, I can do that – because I didn't write a list.

Some cards won't find places, so I put them in a holding deck. Don't throw anything away – things look very different when you try to write them close up, or you might change your mind about something and need a different development. In which case, if you look through the cards you might already have thought of it.

To assess an existing draft

You could use this method to assess a manuscript you've already written, or partially written. I developed it when I had a much-cherished novel in a drawer and I wanted to straighten it out structurally. Then I wished I'd done the cards game with it when I wrote it in the first place.

The ending

The most effective endings are surprising but inevitable. They don't just happen, they have to be designed. The cards game allows you to do this. But some people begin writing without knowing where the story will end, and prefer to see where the characters and situations take them. I think that's risky as you're more likely to lose your way or write an ending that isn't as strong as it could be. And remember, if you leave a blank you are more likely to grind to a halt.

Thumbnail notes... **the end and closure**
> A good ending is not just the knotting of loose ends and the solving of problems. It is also resolution – what psychologists call closure. No more can be done, or no more needs to be done. This is an emotional state as well as an event.
>
> The scenes you choose for the end will create a particular emotional tone, and sometimes if you're having trouble working out your ending it can help to think about the mood you want to create. It might be:
> Triumph – *they got out and it's so good to be alive*
> Healing – *he left her and she was relieved*
> Regret – *it was the saddest story I've ever heard*
> Catharsis – *Manderley burned down which was terrible but now everyone could move on*.

The next step

You can write your first draft straight from the deck of cards – in which case, go to Task 6, The First Draft, on page 79. If you still want to do some playing, or you want to ease into the characters and the world more gradually, now's the time to do a detailed synopsis.

Task 5 Detailed synopsis

This is where you start putting together the details of the story for the first time.

I got used to doing a detailed synopsis for my ghostwriting, where the plot had to be approved by publisher and the 'author' whose name was on the cover. I would meet the publisher and 'author' to kick around ideas, then work them into a detailed outline.

I balked at it at first, not wanting to kill the creative spark, but in fact I found it useful. It allowed me to think in more detail about how I would do things. I could gather together the thoughts I'd had about my characters, their world and what was going to happen and organise them before I had to bring them to life. Otherwise I might come to a direction like *Jenny's wallet goes missing* and have no idea how that might happen.

To start with, take the cards and write the story in order. Then put the cards aside and start to clothe the skeleton. If you've been saving up details about jungle appendicectomies this is where you organise them.

I hop around the story, putting in bits as I think of them – the description of the hero's house, then the party where the climactic confrontation happens.

I find this patchwork approach loosens my creativity although you can do it in chronological order if you wish.

Many more details will start to emerge on their own, and because you've got the structure from the cards game, you have proper places to put them.

Writing style for this synopsis

Don't worry about the writing style. This document is not for anyone else to read. I actually write my synopsis in a colloquial, conversational style, as though I'm explaining the story verbally to a friend. (Imagine saying in your head *there's this bit where a lion's looking at him and he thinks if I ever get out of this alive ...* And so on). This style encourages me to make the scene vivid and interesting. And to excise what's dull.

This document is not the 'selling' synopsis you'll write later when you are introducing the story to the outside world. That requires a specific style of writing and has to be a certain length.

The synopsis you're writing now is for your own comfort, use and support. It can be as long or as short as you like, written any way you want. It's the underwear of the book. Not for anyone's eyes but your own, or those of your most trusted confidantes.

A narrative voice might start to emerge. If so, hooray, every day this novel is getting stronger. Characters also will start to scintillate and develop more traits of their own. As you look at the details more, themes will emerge. You may want to develop these by noting that a scene should have a particular mood, or should stress a particular action.

What's your inner critic doing?

Quite a lot. You want to know if the content is working. If elements are repetitive, dull, predictable. If you need to think of more twists. Like a dot picture, some things look totally different up close.

Now you've firmed up some details, it might be better to have the theft of the wallet discovered early instead of later. You'll need to change things, perhaps the order of events. Try it, see what it does to the rest of the structure. You can play around because you know you have the elements of beginning, middle and end in there. And you may think of better ones as you go along.

What's it ignoring?

The writing style. That doesn't matter at all, nobody will see this document.

Case study: Sorting out a muddle of repetition

I was recently writing a detailed synopsis and it helped me pep up a sequence of numbing monotony. The character had had his memory wiped. The cards went, *Ed does this and this, Friend tells Ed he's done this before*, *Ed wakes up knowing nothing,* and *Ed goes to the archives and discovers it all again.*

It's blindingly obvious now that that's not very interesting. But because I had so many other things to think about when I did the cards I didn't see. The penny dropped, though, when I found I was sketching out the same scene over and over.

After a bit of head-scratching I had an idea. What if the book started further into the story? Then the background could be part of the mystery that the character has to uncover. I got excited.

But wait. Would that work? Would that be too difficult for the reader to follow? All the rest of the story was designed around the original order.

It looked like my brainwave could get me in a deep tangle. Did I want to re-order everything when I'd got a semi-working version?

So I made a new version of the file, did some rough cutting, pasting and dragging, stood back and admired. Much better. The flabby repetitive stuff had gone. And the story was now far more intriguing – there was more to discover about the character's life.

The wind now in my sails, I made several other changes and really honed the story structure. Putting the details in – in effect starting to decorate the walls of the house – allowed me to see repeated material that hadn't been clear before. If I'd gone straight from cards to first draft, it would have been far harder to unpick. And possibly I wouldn't have had the heart to.

Keep your old versions

Every time you make a significant change, preserve your earlier version. There are two reasons. One is that you might make everything worse and want to undo it. The other is more optimistic, or even artistic.

One of the qualities that disappears with constant refining is the raw energy and spirit. Terry Gilliam spent several years rewriting the script for *The Defective Detective*, becoming progressively more disillusioned with it, before unearthing an old version and discovering it was the closest to what he originally intended.

So much in a novel depends on getting the nuances right, and scenes working in relation to other scenes. I often find as I change things, the earlier version is in fact more suitable.

You may also find you have elements that you wanted to get in but can't find room for. Perhaps they repeat other material, or they simply don't fit. Put them in another folder – I call mine the Outtakes file. Don't junk them, particularly if they are repetitions. You never know if later on they will be just perfect.

Do this also if you significantly rewrite a sequence.

Task 5½ Let it settle

Before you go any further you need to check the synopsis works. That there aren't any glaring holes or sequences of meaningless sludge.

Despite all your preparation, major flaws are still possible – even expected.

The only way to judge this is if you have forgotten most of the details. So when you think you've got it right, take a break. Don't do anything on it for couple of weeks. A month is better.

You may well find many reasons to simply plough on. You've got a head of steam and want to write the first draft. You don't want to break your routine or get out of the habit. You're having to snatch the time to write, steal it from other parts of your life and you don't want to waste it. Or you've got a publisher clamouring to see evidence that you have been working, not dreaming.

Sometimes when I've ghosted novels there hasn't been time for me to put the book away. But when I have, I've made huge improvements. Even though I was convinced I had made it as good as I possibly could.

So stop working on the book. If you keep having ideas, jot them down, but in a separate file. Don't you dare open the synopsis file. Its contents are meant to be a surprise when you next read them. Really, this break will pay for itself.

Use the time to do something else writerly. Read. I get on with another book – and maybe you want to try that too. You might be surprised at what happens if you tinker. When your head has been filled with something completely different for a while, go back.

Task 5¾ Assessing the synopsis

Read through your synopsis again. You'll find surprisingly good bits – which you were glad you were distanced enough to see. You'll also spot some howlers you cannot believe you missed.

As you read, check the following points.

The overall impression, how it works as a whole
Are there enough ups and downs, twists and turns? If a story is a straightforward journey from A to B then C with no surprises, that's hardly worth telling. It's known as a linear plot – too predictable.

If you were telling it out loud to a friend, they'd be asleep.

You might want to assess this by gut instinct, or find ways to test your story more rigorously. I like to get creative with the way I do that too – I draw graphs, singling out story strands and characters' journeys. That way the thrills and spills are obvious in an instant, and I can see if they're generally building to a crescendo.

Other writers use music staves, as it gives them a way of representing several story strands, or sub plots, together.

Untapped potential

Sometimes it will be clear that a pair of characters complement each other. One may show the flipside of the other, or a character's possible fate if they carry on as they are.

In Daphne du Maurier's *Rebecca*, the embittered housekeeper Mrs Danvers is in some ways a projection of a possible future for the second Mrs de Winter. And she is also the spokesperson in this world for the dead Rebecca.

A parallel like that might become obvious to you now when it wasn't before. You might want to let it work its way out in the actual writing, or you might want to see if you could take it further.

The way I do it is write lists comparing the characters and drawing parallels to see if there are any I can adjust or add. Now I bet you're glad you did as I suggested and took a break.

You might also find it useful to look at your earliest versions of the story. Remember Terry Gilliam. Sometimes earlier versions, rough though they are, remind you of your original vision.

Aims recap for Tasks 1-5¾

What are you trying to get right at this stage?
A sound story with a beginning, middle and end. And
unexpected turns in the middle. A well-fleshed world
that you're dying to inhabit. Characters who are ready to
act as individuals and who will hopefully evolve even
more as you let them play their parts.

If your novel was a movie, the work you've done so far
has got you to the stage where you're ready to start
shooting.

You're now ready to start creating the actual book.

3 The first draft

The first draft nightmare

This is probably the stage you've been fidgeting to start.
At last we're really writing. It is also the phase that
most professionals put off for as long as possible. If
you've tried to write a novel before, the first draft is the
stage you're most likely to have tried. And possibly
you'll have an inkling why the professionals make such
a fuss.

Some people love the first draft. Certainly it's a thrill to immerse yourself in a world you've created, feel it grow and the characters develop. There's certainly a lot to recommend it, but many of us don't find the first draft quite that easy.

If you don't believe me, google 'first draft' and see how many websites you find full of writers agonising about it and sharing their tips for taking the pain away. One tells of a writing course where on the first day students were given a stern pep talk about how everyone hates their own first drafts but it's just something they have to get on with. You might also find National Novel-Writing Month (NaNoWriMo), an annual cyber-event where participants support each other as they blitz through their first draft. They spend the other 11 months of the year psyching themselves up to it too (or sorting out what they wrote in their state of blind frenzy). And quite a number of these valiant souls don't make it all the way through.

So what's all the fuss about?

The reason first drafts seem to be so difficult is that there's a big gap between expectations and reality. Up until this point we have been nurturing a vision of a brilliant novel. Even if we haven't planned it very thoroughly on paper, the version in our heads is warm, twinkling and faultless. But when we try to write it doesn't come out that way.

This is because for most mortals getting it all right in this stage is impossible.

My first drafts offend my every sensibility. Too long, no pace, clumsy writing, obvious scenes, clunky dialogue, repetition, deviation, hesitation. If you saw them you would think I was not capable of reading, let alone writing. In a first draft we feel we're writing rubbish – and we probably are.

The truth is, few authors write elegant first drafts, no matter how beautiful their finished novels are.

But they do finish them. Remember what I said on p25: writing is rewriting. Revising, editing and polishing.

This means the first draft is not the novel. It is a draft – something to change and work with. Yes, the words you write are no longer signposts and directions. They are the text that will be read by others.

But nobody gets to read it yet. This draft is another development phase.

What a first draft is – guided dreaming

In a first draft, you are bringing the story to life, moment by moment, so that it reads like a novel and not a summary, or notes, or a list.

That's why this stage is like guided dreaming. In a real dream, the right side of your brain goes on a journey with the information it gathered during the day and all the little thoughts you didn't realise you'd had. You don't worry about the content.

Your dreaming brain doesn't get stuck and it doesn't censor. It's a private experience; it doesn't have to please an audience. It explores and often surprises. There will be rubbish, but there will also be moments of sublime inspiration and crazy invention.

In the first draft phase, you are trying to reproduce this process of effortless experience. You are living the story, moment by moment. Making the scenes play to full length for the first time, taking the characters through their thought processes so they do what they have to do.

For the moment, the left, critical, brain is asleep. Questions of good and bad will be dealt with later.

The first draft requires a certain amount of endurance, like a marathon. But writers who warm up their story with thorough preparation find that the first draft flows a lot faster than writers who start cold. As you may have found if you've already tried a first draft and stumbled to a halt.

The first draft is not the finished novel. It's the lucid dream you're having of your novel.

What are you trying to get right at this stage?

You're going to play out your story at its proper length. Immerse yourself in the world. Try to get the scenes as fully realised as possible. Invent the rooms they take place in, the physical details of the characters and what it's like to be in a room with them.

You're going to invite those characters to live in your head. Share their experiences. Write out every syllable of what your people say and how they feel. You're going to use the research you've been doing and integrate it into the experience of your book.

The draft you end up with will be roughly the length of the finished work. Your book will no longer be an embryo. It will be fully grown to its adult height.
But it should be rough. Not just to prove you've bested your inner critic. In the next stage you will be doing a lot more critical work and you need to be prepared to change things.

That's a lot easier if it's rough than if you have tried to make it perfect.

What are you ignoring for now?

You are ignoring a lot. Although your book will be full length it will not be mature. It will need more stages of analysis and rewriting. Close your ears to any niggling voices that tell you, this is bad.

In particular, ignore the writing style and the narrative voice. If a narrative voice comes to you naturally, all the better. But don't sweat it. Your job at this stage is to mine your imagination and be spontaneous. Do not stifle that. Go with the flow.

Some days you will feel like writing in a certain style, others another style will come most naturally. Embrace these differences; they are part of the process of discovery. And they are helping you to 'live' the scenes, which is the ultimate goal of this phase.

However, sometimes your inner critic will suggest a better way to do a scene, or that you need an additional element in the plot, and you'll be grateful. But don't let it start looking for problems or things to improve.

Only rewrite if your inner critic is telling you immediately, NOW, what to do. If it doesn't, leave the offending passage and press on.

Break up the order

No one says you have to write your book in strict chronological order. Some writers start at the end and write their way back to the beginning. Or they write one complete plot strand, getting completely immersed in all its possibilities and the personalities involved. When that's done, they write another complete strand, and another. Then they chop them all together like a rough-cutting a movie.

Write one day, edit the next

You may want to write on one day, then edit on the next. I don't do this because I prefer to edit all in one go. The book evolves as I write and before I edit I reassess the whole thing. For me, editing as I go along is a waste of time. But if you must neaten as you go, you must. Just don't try to write and edit a scene at the same time. That's when you're most likely to get stuck.

Task 6 The first draft

Mental weapons for the first draft

1: How to tell your inner critic it's not wanted

Do you still think you might find it difficult to leave things when you know they're ropey? This is how to force your left brain to switch off.

Leave the misspellings and typos uncorrected. This makes you ignore the things you already know are a bit wrong in other ways.

In fact, but for making sure my fingers are hitting roughly the right keys, I don't even look at what I'm typing. It's the closest thing to writing with eyes closed. If my touch-typing was that good that's what I'd do. If you're having a think about something, you don't censor the language you're using in your head. If you're dreaming, you let it flow. That's the ideal state you get into with the first draft.

Disregarding the typos is an important way to persuade my brain that I am not trying to produce the finished work. Literals are screaming at you, in red and green wiggly lines. Refuse to see them, and it turns down your critical radar for everything. You just get on and write.

So be a detail slob. And make your inner critic roll its eyes and give up.

2: Recognise when the inner critic breaks through
The inner critic is bound to break through from time to time, such is the nature of marathons. To tackle it, we borrow from sports psychology.

Learn to recognise when you are undermining your own performance. Then learn to react to it in a positive way. This is also the basis of cognitive behaviour therapy, which, in a nutshell, identifies patterns of 'stinking thinking' – how your own thoughts make a tricky situation far worse than it needs to be. Successful writers know how to deal with the inner voice of doubt.

On bad days, this is what might be going through my head. Chances are, it will be going through your head too.

- Scenes are going on too long
- Scenes are unexciting
- Characters are all sounding the same
- What I thought would take moments to write has taken all morning
- In the synopsis, this scene was going to be brilliant. Why have I messed it up?
- It's all rubbish

You should by now know what the answer is to these points. Repeat after me: *So what? There is a time for sorting that out later. Not now. We carry on.*

There are two other saboteurs you might encounter.

- There's a small logistical problem I can't get my head around
- I can't get into it today

These last two are types of block and I've got a whole arsenal of tools for them. See Block busters, p91.

Be prepared for the doubt days and how you will feel. Also know your experience is not unusual. It's like that for most of us. Other writers are with you every step of the agony.

Of course, there are also days when you hit your stride. Or maybe you'll always find it easy. In which case you can sit back and snigger at how most of us manage to make it very hard for ourselves.

Writing rules for the first draft

Thumbnail notes... Show not tell

Writing your first draft requires a different mindset from the one you've probably been using for the planning stages.

There's a dramatic principle called show not tell, which you may have heard of.

Showing a scene involves the reader and gives them an experience. It enacts it. If an event is presented this way we remember it. *Telling* is more distancing, less involving and harder for the reader to remember. It's like smuggling a statement into the small print instead of drawing attention to it.

Let me give an example. *Jenny finds her wallet and is horrified*. That's telling. It's short and it's over in one line.

You may want this development to be largely ignored, of course, in which case, keep it in the small print. If you want it to be more memorable, try this instead.

Jenny opened the glove compartment. The breakdown number must be here somewhere. She poked her hand in, swept aside the tampons, box of travel sweets. Petrol receipts, Trudie's old mobile and…A black leather wallet with one red jeweled button.

Jenny reached in and pulled it out. Her thumb eased the clip open from long familiarity, a movement as automatic to her as opening her own front door. Because it was her wallet. Here in Trudie's car.

She took a long, deep breath and checked the bill slot. It was, to her complete lack of surprise, empty.

She became aware of a sharp rapping at the window. A strange man with his hair cut too short like a shorn GI was standing at the window. For a moment she wondered who he was, then saw that in his hand was an official-looking piece of paper. Of course, the driver of the other car. In the shock she had forgotten all about the accident. For now, the fuss of having to exchange insurance details seemed like less hassle than what she had just discovered …

It's rough and it's not going to win any prizes, but I hope you can see the difference. The second version is the scene playing out in front of the reader's eyes, with the reader sharing the experience. That's showing, not telling.

Your synopsis will probably be written in the telling mode, because that is what we naturally do when we summarise. It's easy to remain in 'tell' mode when you're using the synopsis to give you directions. I constantly have to remind myself because the 'voice' of the synopsis is infectious. Now you are inhabiting a scene and the characters' viewpoints you need to make a mental switch.

If you're finding a scene is not proving as vivid as you thought it might, this could be what's going wrong. Slow down, and imagine it step by step. If you find you're stuck in a summarising frame of mind, there are various ways to break out. You could try the creative game in the section on block busters, What comes next, p95. Or use the soundtrack technique, p102.

Showing instead of telling doesn't mean you have to make the scene long, by the way. You don't even have to write it blow by blow. What it means is that you present it with tangible detail so it is memorable. Although for now, try not to précis. Editing is for later.

Rule 1: Be long-winded

Imagine all the detail you possibly can. You will probably end up with far too much material, but this is the best time to conjure it up. For the first time you are living the novel more vividly than you ever have before. You are shooting material from which you will make the final cut. Like rushes from a movie, some scenes will be far, far too long. That gives you plenty of scope for later.

Rule 2: Be obvious

Don't try to be subtle. Maybe good, finished novels in your genre are subtle and oblique and have subtexts and layers of literary parallels. But these qualities can only be assessed by considering the manuscript as a whole, which you cannot do right now.

One of the biggest mistakes novice writers make is to try to be too subtle. They do it in the first draft, and then they tone it down even further. The result? No reader can fathom what's going on.

So in this draft make your characters' intentions very plain. Make it crystal clear what they want. Signal your plot developments in an obvious way. Underline significant events so that nobody misses them. And do not worry about it.

Being obvious will also clarify these things in your own mind. How will you expect the reader to understand the true 'meaning' of a plot development or the purpose of scene if you don't?

So, no subtlety, please. If you start off trying to be subtle, it will inhibit you and drive you further into a swamp of hidden meaning. This is the stage to put everything in neon lights. You can decide how far to turn it down later.

Rule 3: Don't be inhibited

A significant problem with first drafts is that the writer censors themselves emotionally. It's very hard to get used to revealing emotions when in real life we keep them private.

But novels often show their characters' private moments, and so emotion is what readers want. And they want these emotions enacted – a novel is an experience, not an analysis.

Of course, your characters won't be operatically emoting the whole time. That would exhaust the reader and it is totally unbelievable. Sometimes they'll be cool, dismissive, having a laugh.

But there will – or should – be moments in your story when people will have to really reveal what's in their hearts. That's what I'm talking about.

Don't worry that the love scene you are writing may look overblown or silly. This draft is the time you let go of your inhibitions.

It doesn't matter if you make a fool of yourself. Nobody will stare at you, or even know it was done. Nobody will see the scene but you, when you revise. And that will be with the sole intention of deciding what you will do with the gush.

If you're embarrassed about writing something but it has to be in the story, dig deep and get on with it. If you don't mine the emotional depth of a scene or a situation at this stage, you may not be able to at all later, when the critical faculties are standing there smirking with their arms folded.

There are a number of things you might find yourself doing instead of getting emotionally engaged with a scene. You might rush the writing so you've got it done.

You might tell instead of show. Both of these techniques preserve a safe distance.

But this draft is not meant to be safe, you're meant to get a bit extreme and go to places you've never been. Take a risk.

You cannot be inhibited in this phase. You must go for full-blown operatic drama. This is where you live the book in Technicolor, not in washed out tones. You want it to take on a life of its own, be a bit crazy if it wants to be.

Rule 4: Be bold and try things
Hollywood writers talk about squeezing the lemon. By this they mean getting the most drama out of a situation, character or theme. The most entertainment value.

Whenever you find a lemon (dramatic situation), squeeze it. Hard. See how far you can push the tension or the comedy of a scene. See if a character might do something desperate or outrageous. Send them that little bit further than you envisaged in the synopsis.

This is a rough draft, you're allowed to go OTT. You might get rubbish. Or nudging the scene over the edge might tip it into something gripping.

Rule 5: If you decide later on to change something
Formal rewrites are not allowed at this phase. But sometimes you just know something earlier in the book

has to be changed, or you need to lay the foundations for a plot development.

If you do have to go back, keep your revision rough. Do not attempt to write it nicely and in pretty prose. That will get you into the wrong mindset. It will also tempt you to start sorting out all the other offensivenesses you spot and then you will really be derailed. Ignore any other mistakes you see. Revel in the roughness.

Similarly, if you have to write a whole new section, zip it down and drop it in. Don't worry about joining it up neatly, that's for later.

How to deviate without losing your way

The first draft is a process of evolution. Your novel is under new management now – the management of your right brain. Your synopsis is not a straitjacket. Allow yourself to change things.

If new ideas are hammering on the door, let them in and see if you like the look of them. If a scene pulls you somewhere it's not supposed to, don't chop it off immediately. Allow yourself to go with it for, say, five minutes, then resolve that you'll go back to what you were supposed to be doing. This is how stories develop, characters take over.

As characters start to come alive, things change. Despite all the synopsising, there are certain scenes that don't work out the way you thought. Some situations that may be impossible because you now realise the characters would not do those things.

Usually, though, they still fit quite well with what you've planned.

But what if your brainwave changes things far more radically? Is your synopsis redundant?

No. It is still a valuable working document. Don't abandon it and strike off into the wilderness. Keep on top of the job and rework the synopsis.

The exception is if the sudden realisation of the 'true' direction has armed you with enough confidence to fly without the synopsis. Some writers do work like this – and the moment they abandon the plan is when they feel they have truly connected with the book.

Going off piste like this is risky – but if you can do it, great.

But some writers feel like the synopsis has abandoned *them*, that it was all a waste of time. Not so. Adapt your synopsis and carry on. If you try to battle on without it you are just as likely to get lost as if you set off without a synopsis in the first place.

And don't feel that all your previous work was wasted. All those hours of planning, conceptualising and drafting are what got you to this nuclear blast of inspiration. Be profoundly grateful for it and forge ahead with renewed vigour.

Writer's block

First draft is the biggest danger time for writer's block –
or not knowing what to write next.

You don't get writer's block in the planning stages.
When you hit a blank there, you go for a walk or read a
few books and the idea will come to you. It's all a lot
less formal. The empty screen isn't scary at that stage.

When an empty screen is scary and blocking is the first
draft.

There are two reasons why blocks happen in the first
draft. One is that you think you're writing rubbish – and
we've already dealt with that.

The other reason is that you hit a blank in the plot.

In the first draft you have to solve a lot of small-scale
snags that you may not have thought about before. *They
escape*, you wrote blithely in your plan. Now you've got
to invent the way they escape.

Suddenly that's an enormous problem. It can keep you
tied in knots for hours. Up until now, you have been able
to ignore such details, but in the first draft you can't.

All published writers get days like this, but they work
through them. If they really don't know what to do with
a particular scene, they just close their eyes and start
writing. Something – anything – that will turn those
trapped characters into escaped characters.

And what's going to be the worst that can happen? You write something that's not very good. You already know it's not a capital offence. Who's going to see? But usually as you grope your way through a random solution, a much better one comes along.

The blank spot might not always be a plot solution. Other kinds of blanks might be:

- how to get a scene to reveal a crucial piece of information
- a writerly hunch that the pacing or balance will be wrong if you dive straight into the next episode in your synopsis
- a feeling that what you have written in your synopsis is not good enough – *They escape* looks predictable. Of course *they* have to *escape* or the story will end right there. In that case, the nature of your block is how to make the escape surprising in some way.

There's another type of block. A character says 'when did you last see him?' and you have to decide. Was it two days ago? Five weeks? This can produce mad, staring paralysis as you try to unravel the consequences of each possibility. But the timeline – who did what and when – is one of those housekeeping things you can sort out later. For now, write something magnificently vague such as 'last week' or 'last year' and sail on. (More on timeline on p106.)

For all the others, you're suddenly on the spot. You have to invent something and you've dried up.

Nora Roberts puts it rather well: 'If I've written crap I can do something about it. If I walk away and leave a blank page, I can't do anything about that.' She has published more than 200 novels.

If you've got stuck like this your muse has not deserted you. It can't after all that work you've done. But sometimes your muse hides just around the corner and you have to keep trudging until you catch up with it again. I have always found that if I just keep going, it starts to work itself out. First of all I realise what I don't want the scene to be, and that starts to give me clues to what I do want.

So – you don't get blocked. You keep writing and you leave no gaps. And anyway, if you've prepared, these hitches are small scale.

Block busters

Block buster 1: Just write at random
The most straightforward block buster is just to write. I write anything, I try things. I let the characters yammer away like actors improvising a scene, saying nonsense and seeing what happens. Most of it is pointless, it goes round and round and gets deleted instantly. I keep going until something new has happened or been said.

Since we're bring random, you could bring some other contributors into the mix. Tarot cards might suggest characters or events. Googling a word at random can be surprisingly productive if you can discipline yourself not to go on a four-hour browsing spree instead. Just add a new element, play with it and see where it takes you.

Block buster 2: Reincorporation
Remember the discussion about plotting and reincorporation in section 1 (p57)? Instead of adding new material, you solve your problem using a character, trait, event or piece of information that you casually introduced earlier.

Was one of your characters out of the house one evening, and did you randomly decide they were at choir practice? If you brought that in again in some way, would that get you out of your hole? Or if you changed the choir practice to locksmithing evening class, would that be a satisfactory way to help your trapped characters escape?

You might have to do a little retrospective editing here – in which case, remember to keep it rough.

Block buster 3: Conflict
Remember the discussion on conflict in section 1 (p39)? It's a good way to spice up a scene that's predictable, or to slip in a piece of information the reader needs to know.

Block buster 4: Get your hands on something else
Your brain will gush with ideas as soon as you are unable to write them down. If you don't believe me, go and make meatballs. Just when your hands are nicely

slimed and in no fit state to touch a pen, you will be overwhelmed with inspiration.

Less messily, some writers I know always have some knitting on the go, and when they're stuck they pick up the needles.

There's something about taking your hands off the keyboard and doing something technical that sends the ideas flooding into your brain.

I remember one book I was ghosting where I was working on a scene that involved a lot of technical information. The characters were trekking through deep jungle with only a map and compass. I am a dunce about direction; the limits of my understanding are up and down. I don't even do right and left. East and west were giving me a panicky feeling. And as for the compass bearings and ridge lines... Worse, I had to make the characters do exciting things while showing their mastery of this information. I was getting close to acute prostration.

Like a frustrated schoolchild, my brain kept interrupting with impure thoughts. That pair of jeans I was thinking about customising. Wouldn't they look nice with a design drawn on them. Oh please, no more about bearings and ridge lines. Hmm, a design. What design? Pretty soon, although I had no idea about what to do about the ridge lines, I had the design for the jeans, plus a method for how I'd measure and rough it out so that it looked right. The brain, if given a task, is wonderfully inventive at concentrating on something else.

The call was too strong. I spent an hour with marker pens and tape measures, during which time the two tasks in my head were reversed. My brain knew what it had to do about the jeans, in fact was bored thinking about it. I found my thoughts wandering to the wretched navigation scene and returned to my desk refreshed. (And I was very proud of the jeans.)

The ideal diversion activity is something that doesn't require too much creative invention. Clothes altering or mending, although creative, requires a lot of repetitive sewing or unpicking.

Some people get a lot of hoovering done during their first drafts. If you are doing a task that's dull but technical, your brain craves something to think about – and you can often solve a problem effortlessly.

Block buster 5: Improv games
The brain comes up with ideas much better as soon as you stop pressuring it to. Diversion activities help with this, but they have a drawback – it may look to the rest of the family as if you have stopped working and are available for interruptions. Or you might already have hoovered until the carpets are bald.

So I've adapted a series of improvisational theatre games to play while you are actually writing, and help break the block.

The added bonus is that while you're playing the game, you're actually writing the scene.

These games, adapted from Keith Johnstone's *Impro for Storytellers*, are another kind of mental diversion. They give your brain something to do besides getting words down. You focus on obeying the rules instead of worrying about what you are inventing.

Of course, the result looks odd on the page, but you are not going to leave the passages like this. You are doing these tasks to get your creative juices flowing. Limits often make you more creative, not less. If you held a dinner party where all the food was white, you would have to use far more ingenuity than if you could serve any old thing from Nigel or Nigella. The chances are that your 'white' menu will have far more panache than you could imagine was possible.

Creativity sees boundaries and tries to bust out of them. And often I find I can stop one of these games half-way through because I've had a good idea for what I really want to do.

Game 1 *What comes next*

The first game is to slow down a brain that is panicking because the problem looks far too complicated to solve.

In the stage version the actor is told what to do by members of the audience. They are allowed to tell him just one action at a time, such as 'you take off your shoe'.

The actor does that but THAT ONLY. He doesn't take off the sock as well, or his hat, or the other shoe.

Because that may not be the next thing he does. He waits to be told what happens next.

It might be: 'you look inside'. Then: 'You see a spider. ' 'You scream.' 'The spider screams back.'

Or it might be: 'a note falls out.' 'You pick up the note.' 'It says, take off the other shoe first.'

Simple stuff, but where I find this useful is that it slows down a galloping, panicking brain. You are not allowed to think of more than one thing at a time (so cannot summarise) and you pay attention to the detail of what's going on. You stop trying to complicate things.

Over-complicating a task is one of the biggest ways to lose confidence and end up in a mess. But writers (and artists too), cannot help but see connections between the most unlikely things – at times their creative faculties are their own worst enemy. When this gets out of control, you are paralysed with choice.

So slow down, take the scene step by step, and see how it comes out. Slip in a surprising thing and see what happens.

Game 2 *Three-word sentences*
Every sentence you write has to be three words long.

In the stage version, instead of saying 'Come in,' the actors have to say 'Darling come in'. Instead of 'What's up' they might have to say 'Are you upset?'

Both these phrases imply a relationship between the characters and make the actors open up to each other more. The only other rule is that each sentence must be complete.

On stage, this game is about dialogue and making it reveal more about the characters and the story. But you can use it when writing scenes without dialogue too. I find constraints such as this unlock creative potential as I start to think of ingenious ways to make sensible three-word sentences that take the scene where I need it to go.

You might want to vary the number – try nine-word sentences. See what it does to your brain and the kind of things you have to invent. They will be things you wouldn't have thought of normally.

You could also try throwing a die to see how long to make the next sentence.

Game 3: *No S*
This is self-explanatory. It forces you to find other ways of writing things. Choose any letter you like, of course. Or, in a dialogue scene, forbid one character to use S, one to use E and so on. It gets you thinking about what they really want to say.

Game 4: *Verse and worse*
Even more self-explanatory. Try madrigals. Or rap. You don't have to be good at them – I'm not, but I'll try anything in the privacy of my own first draft.

And if you're like me, you'll soon be glad to give up and write straight prose again.

Game 5: *Emotional goals*
This helps if you feel a scene is not interesting enough. In the stage version, the scene starts with the players feeling one emotion and having to progress to another. So, they're driving through the forest at night and their mood has to shift from 'happy to sad', or 'frightened to confident'.

In your novel, this could be a very useful game to play. Pick an emotion at random and concentrate on making the change to it gradually with the situation you've got. If, half-way through, you realise the progression should be the other way around, so much the better.

By experimenting with something you don't want, you realise what the true scene should be. Your choice of emotions doesn't even have to be sensible – it could be a bit absurd, such as 'horrified to hungry'.

Although don't get too whacky. It might be hard to get anything useful out of 'grateful to green'.

How to keep yourself at the desk

The actual writing is an up-and-down process. Some days it'll go beautifully. Others, even with all your preparation, are a total slog.

This is not block. This is just not being in the mood.

Professionals carry on anyway – they usually have deadlines. Hobby writers don't have that pressure. But usually they don't want to waste hard-earned writing time either.

Here's how to make the difficult days productive, so that writing is routine even when you don't feel like doing it.

Targets
It helps to have targets. A minimum number of words done per session, then you're allowed to stop. Some writers like to keep this target ridiculously low. Graham Greene used to write a mere 500, although he was editing as he went along. But he stopped at 500, no matter whether it was the middle of a scene or even a sentence.

There's certainly something to be said for setting yourself goals that aren't going to frighten you. It may be a slow way to proceed – but it is sure. Personally I like to see a manuscript grow faster than that, but I am a rewriter, restructurer, fiddler. Graham Greene aimed to get it perfect first time.

There's also something to be said for stopping mid-sentence. Next time you come back the engine's still running.

If targets are your thing, you might find it useful to get a writing buddy who can spur you on. Like Weight

Watchers, if you have to confess your wordcount to others it will soon be clear if you're slipping. This is the principle behind NaNoWriMo, where the goal is to complete 50,000 words in 30 days. That's a tall order, but as you watch your online writing buddies you can see their wordcounts rise. For those of a competitive nature it's a powerful incentive to keep writing.

I don't set myself targets, but I do love wordcounts. So I make a working synopsis.

This is a copy of my synopsis file that I can hack about. I clipboard off the section I'm going to write, put it in my manuscript file and write what's in there at full length. When that's done, I clipboard off the next passage to write. Bit by bit the working synopsis file gets smaller.

This is immensely satisfying as I have two wordcounts to congratulate myself with – the working synopsis and the manuscript itself. And the working synopsis shows me how far through the book I've got, which keeps me focussed on getting to the end.

Writing incentives
- Wordcount targets
- Writing buddies
- Working synopsis

But targets can work against you. They can make you focus on ticking the box, going the distance, or chopping the next bit off the working synopsis file. It's tempting to rush ahead instead of immersing yourself in the scene;

and remember, the aim of the first draft is to show, not tell.

Experience has taught me to see the signs. If I detect I'm glossing over things, if I'm telling instead of dawdling and dreaming, I need help.

Tricks to make you do the work properly

I have three defences against rushing.

Emergency rescue library

I take a quick break and read something. It might be one of my trusty writing textbooks (yes, even full-fledged writers use them, all the time). More commonly for this situation I choose fiction that has a similar prose style to what I am writing. Sometimes non-fiction works too.

I don't have to read very much. Within a few paragraphs I start to enjoy thinking 'up close' instead of getting my quota done.

Good writing always makes me want to write something myself and I am easily infected by someone else's style. Enjoying how someone else has noticed details and used them lulls me into a suitable mental rhythm. And it reminds me that I enjoy what I'm doing, that there is such pleasure in invention. I return to my work refreshed.

It's not copying, because I'm so strongly anchored to my story that the content is totally different. But absorbing the rhythms of a like-minded writer makes me think of the kind of things my characters might say, or how my emerging narrative voice might sound.

What you write after this might be a bit different from the rest of the book. That doesn't matter – the style of the first draft is rough, you discover its true voice at a later stage. You'll find when you look through the first draft that the style varies vastly from day to day, with or without the odd madrigal. The point of this exercise is to get your imagination into a productive frame of mind.

I wouldn't do this on a rewrite because the tone is vital then – every word and nuance counts. But for the first draft, having a few emergency rescue authors is like having a therapist who can put me in a good mood to write again.

A soundtrack for your novel

I used to think I couldn't work if I could hear music. That it would take too much of my attention and influence what I was doing. Then I realised that was a bonus sometimes.

If I've got itchy feet and am rushing to get through my quota, music can keep me in the moment. As soon as I put an album on, I'm content to let it play to the end. That puts me in the frame of mind to let the scene play to its natural end too.

A lot of people write to music. Whole forums are devoted to discussing what they listen to. Film soundtracks are ideal as they're not meant to be centre stage, they're meant to underline story points and moods. Classical is popular too. Some people can't abide anything with lyrics because the words get in the way – although I never find that's a problem.

But sometimes you get interesting results with more attention-grabbing music. Music can make you walk with a swagger in your step – and it can make you write that way too.

I was once struggling with an action climax for a book. This is often the hardest kind of sequence to write in detail. Your synopsis says *There is a struggle*. Suddenly you have to choreograph that struggle blow for blow. Working it out can be tedious.

I knew this would be a tough one and I put Fatboy Slim on the headphones.

The sequence went like a dream. Fatboy's cheeky rhythms were exactly what I needed to make the sequence spring with quirky, entertaining details. His twisty way with samples made me challenge my material and squeeze more fun out of it.

What's more, when I came back to it in the redraft phase, it had energy and fizz. Usually my first drafts of action scenes are detail-perfect but weighed down and slow.

So if music works for you – and it does for most people – build up a soundtrack for your book.

And you don't have to keep the soundtrack for times of trouble. Some days I feel like writing to music, and so I do.

You don't even have to keep it for when you're writing. Put it on in the car or if you're walking about, and enjoy a different way to be thinking about your novel without the pressure to get anything produced.

Use it, too, if you're girding your loins for a rewrite or you've had a break from the novel.

In the writing business, authors often have to go back to a manuscript they put away several months before, for instance when a publisher gives feedback. When this happens to me, I've lost the intense connection I had with the characters and story while I was writing. In fact I can't even imagine ever getting it back. But the soundtrack is the express route to the emotional centre of the novel again.

Play 'what comes next'
This ever-versatile game, p95, reminds you to take the scene one step at a time.

Weapons against rushing
- Look for writers who will pull you back to the right path should you find you are rushing or struggling. Add them to your working library.
- Build a soundtrack for your novel.
- Play 'what comes next'

Other good habits for the first draft

1: Prepare for tomorrow

Reserve time at the end of your writing session to prepare for the next one in a no-pressure way. Think about the next scene you're going to write. Check that you know the objectives, such as making a revelation or putting a character in danger. If you don't have a detailed synopsis, make a few sketchy notes about how the scene will go. Then forget about it. When you come back to they keyboard, your subconscious will have started it already.

2: Make a personal details file

In this draft you're likely to have several physical details you need to keep track of. What people look like, how long it takes to get from one person's house to another, how to fire a bow and arrow.

To remind yourself, you can, of course, look back through the draft. But to do so might give you the vapours. In that case, make separate notes of anything you might have to refer back to.

Each time you establish a description of a place or a character, or decide your hero spent six months living in Dubai, copy it into a file of general descriptions. If you write by hand on paper, keep a notebook handy.

Even if your constitution is made of sterner stuff, there's a good reason to do this. When you look over your manuscript there will be nice surprises as well as fallen souffles, of things that went beautifully. You don't want to tear off the wrapping paper too soon and spoil the freshness.

3: Ignore the timeline

Until the characters act out the story it's not obvious that you need to work out a timeline for the events – who did what and when. You could establish it before you start writing, but the chances are it won't feel that pressing. It's fine to leave it until afterwards.

But don't try to do it as you go along in the first draft. Creating a timeline requires you to analyse the plot as a whole. What were they doing the other night? Was it Sunday?

This is not the way you should be thinking when you're immersed in the writing.

The exception is if a detail like that is crucial to the plot. For instance, the time it would take to drive from Glasgow to Edinburgh on country lanes. If your character simply has to do that, quickly google and stick it in.

But for any detail that's not pivotal – such as a casual 'yesterday' or 'last year' – leave it until later.

When you assess other aspects of the manuscript there's a quick and easy way to check the timeline. Then if you need to do any tweaks (and there are bound to be some) you can include them in the redraft.

4: Use your Outtakes file

Remember the Outtakes file from the first section (p68)? I create one for the first draft too, for a number of reasons.

Sometimes there's a point in the synopsis I decide not to include. Maybe that storyline has evolved differently, or it repeats something already in there. (It's amazing how that won't be clear when you're writing the synopsis, but once you play the scene out in full you see it with absolute certainty.)

I don't junk it, though. The book is still at a rough stage and much may change later on. What I feel won't fit at the moment might fit after some more work's been done. Even if it repeats material that's in there from earlier, keep it. That version may be more suitable than the one you decided to use.

The second type of contribution the Outtakes file gets is the passages that I started writing one particular way and then changed. Or a development that occurred to me on the spur of the moment. The earlier version might prove useful in the redraft, so I keep a copy.

You will end up with a long file full of what seems like rubbish. But it's not rubbish, it's a junk shop of forgotten treasure, although it will need a polish. I have often needed to beef up a plot strand or skew it in a different way, have hunted through the Outtakes file and found I already had it.

Even if you don't use the Outtakes treasures in this book, they might be useful seedlings for a future one. Never throw anything away.

First draft survival strategy

Hopefully, with all this preparation, this phase will go like a dream rather than a nightmare. I have to confess that even with my detailed synopsis and my carefully organised research, I still find first drafts are a peculiar form of torture.

Here's your first draft survival strategy:
- Fling the words down
- Leave all spelling mistakes and typos
- Try to avoid looking back over anything you've done
- Show, don't tell
- Squeeze the lemon
- Make files as you go along where you copy details of character descriptions, house descriptions, where characters went to school, so that you can check consistency without looking through the actual text
- Make an Outtakes file
- Critical editing is generally forbidden, but if you think of a way to do a scene better, do go back and fiddle – but leave it rough

- Don't worry about the timeline, sort that out later
- Use wordcount targets or a writing buddy to keep you focussed
- Make a working plot file, and delete a section each time you've done it. Watch with satisfaction as it dwindles to nothing
- Become aware of when you are rushing
- If music helps you concentrate, assemble a soundtrack for your book
- Have a rescue library to get you in a writing mood
- Don't be afraid to take a short break with a hands-occupying diversion activity
- Play improvisation games if the writing is going through a painful stage

Finally I sweat my way to the end of the first draft, and collapse with gratitude. And you should too. You have passed an important milestone. The novel is now, for the first time, a novel.

Aims recap for Task 6

What are you trying to get right at this stage?

This is still a stage of experimentation. You are staging the book's events in real time, seeing how they feel when you 'live' them. You are converting summaries into scenes. You are exploring its world, squeezing every nuance of drama that you come across and not worrying if it's overdone.

This is where you must explore the full potential for your story and your characters.

You are changing plans when you need to, although you are still always trying to follow a route map. You are getting to know the characters and letting them live. You are creating a full-length version of the book.

You will have a manuscript running to several hundred pages, a satisfying chunk of words. It is by no means perfect but it is a great hurdle. Now you have turned all that work into something significant.

What's your inner critic doing?

Your inner critic is noticing when you're showing not telling. It's spotting when you're hurrying to get a scene over and done with, watching the wordcount instead of living the scene. It's taking remedial action by prescribing some music, reading or therapeutic knitting. It's pointing out when you need to rethink or when a sequence is repetitive.

It's turning a blind eye to everything else.

Task 7 Before you get to work on the novel again

If you wrote a detailed synopsis and took a break as I recommended, I hope you found it worthwhile.

After finishing the first draft, a break is even more important.

If you plunge back in straight away you'll edit for the wrong reasons.

You'll keep passages because you spent so long on them; because you based them on something you liked in a film; because they contain fine phrasing.

You'll delete passages because you cringe at how they read – but you won't know that beyond the clumsy words the content and intent is pure gold.

In short, you will judge the words you used, how you felt when you were writing them and how they do or do not meet your expectations.

But to edit a first draft effectively, you have to forget all this. It's emotional baggage and you need a fresh start. Your novel is now a new entity and you have to form a new relationship with it.

For the ropier sections, you need to decide what to do – and excising them in a flush of embarrassment won't be the answer. You also need to know if your finer passages are suitable for their purpose. At first such a thought will be sacrilege, but it is unlikely that they are absolutely perfect. Only with distance can you tell how to adapt them.

You don't have to sever all contact with the book, though. You can still keep in touch with the world and the characters. Read more in the genre, or explore more books that might be similar. Listen to your soundtrack, just for fun – and see what springs up in your mind. Make notes, perhaps about themes or overall structures that have now become apparent to you.

Don't do anything about your notes yet. Save them for when you pick up the reins again.

You might suddenly have a bolt-like inspiration for a scene. If so, write it roughly and paste it in, but blindfold yourself to anything else around it.

Also, read some books that are totally different. This is meant to be a break.

Stephen King's minimum break period is six weeks, but only you can judge how long you need. Wait until the exact details of what you wrote have faded from your mind. Until you are ready to accept your novel in its new incarnation and get to know it afresh – warts, wonders and all.

Then you're ready for the next stage.

4 Before you rewrite

Remember that perfect vision you had of the novel, months ago when you first started all this? When it was a twinkle in your eye and every new idea you added made it even better? Now, your ideals may be feeling a bit bruised. Eminent misery-gutses keep telling you to build up a tolerance for your own crap.

Well, the time for crap has passed. You can still create an enthralling story that you want to share with others. We're going to fix your novel.

You may be expecting to start rewriting immediately. Get rid of all those clumsy sentences grinding in your writerly ear; the typos creaking on their wiggly red trampolines. Forget those for a little while longer. You won't touch a word of the manuscript until you've gone through another process.

Do you have a sneaky feeling the novel is now not as coherent or controlled as when you wrote your synopsis? If it's gone off piste, that's fine. In fact, rejoice. It's part of the book's evolution. Even if you did stick to the original plan, you probably found that some elements didn't work the way you expected.

To edit your draft effectively, you need to see the book as a whole, not trudge through the forest of words hacking whatever you see. So you don't start editing straight away. First you do another kind of mechanical and structural survey.

What, more procrastination? *Au contraire*, this is valuable work. Like the other planning stages it will make the editing far faster and more productive. It will make the difference between a disorganised, amateur-looking novel and one that works well.

Thumbnail notes...Structure

Good, satisfying novels have sound structure. The individual scenes have more power, because a scene works within the context of a story as well as on its own. Novels whose structure is not robust feel aimless, wander off the point and lose the reader's interest.

Getting the structure of your novel right is the smart way to edit.

Aims

What are you trying to get right at this stage?
You are going to critically assess what you have done. You are not going to write any actual words or alter the manuscript yet. You are going to make a rewriting plan, which will get the most out of your story and your characters. You are going to get the best dramatic value out of your scenes and decide what to cut.

There may be many ways you could make the book go – and you are going to work out which is the right one.

What are you ignoring for now?
Correcting the writing. You won't alter a single word of the manuscript. There's time for all that later.

You also ignore your original plan. Your novel has evolved and outgrown your original synopsis. It has hauled itself out of the sea and developed legs and wings. It is a new creature.

What a first draft looks like

Brace yourself –your inner critic is about to give you a good lashing. Here are the typical things it will say:

- some scenes are too long or too short
- the characterisation is rough, and varies wildly from start to finish
- the pace is inconsistent, either relentlessly fast or monotonously slow
- the timeline is totally random and one week has several Thursdays
- the themes don't come through
- the writing doesn't sparkle (and if you've been following my recommendations to the letter, the spelling, grammar etc are execrable too)
- the dramatic scenes lack impact
- the dialogue is obvious
- irrelevant nonsense has crept in
- characters have run away with certain scenes or threads
- the tone is uneven and seems to belong to several separate books, and then there are the unexplained madrigals

You may be wondering why you did all that preparation if what you end up with is so rough. But you have just transformed a document of perhaps 10 or 20 pages (if you did a detailed synopsis) into several hundred. You have a lot of material to work with.

As well as the roughness, there will also be scenes of sublime invention and blissful rightness. Because you took a break you are now able to see them.

If you've been polishing as you go along, you will still have most of these problems and the book won't work much better than if you had left it rough. (That's why I leave the prettifying stage until later.)

You could assess your novel by reading it and making long lists, but I've developed a method that's far easier and produces a document that serves the purpose better than a list. Even better, it's fun.

It's time for another creative game. The beat sheet.

Task 8 The beat sheet game

In Hollywood, scriptwriters break down a story into a summary they call a beat sheet. I've adapted this for my novels and it's immensely useful.

The beat sheet lets you check all of the story mechanics. You use it to answer the following critical questions.
- Has my novel got enough highs and lows?
- Do I have too many scenes on the same emotional note?
- Should I slip in a quieter scene to give the reader a breather from the tension, or perhaps a bit of humour?
- Do I need more tension or suspense?
- Is the opening gripping, and true to the story (don't write a thriller-type opening if the rest of the novel is going to proceed at a much quieter pace)
- Is the ending satisfying? Is it surprising yet inevitable? Does it properly answer the question

set by the story? Do I need to plant more seeds to make it work?

- If it's a thriller, is it pacy enough?
- If it's a comedy, have I got enough laughs?
- Have I given the prominence I want to the characters who are most interesting?
- Does one character monopolise the story, and do I want it that way?
- Has the sub-plot (if there is one) taken over or dried away completely?
- Are there any other loose ends?
- Does my sub-plot relate to the main plot or has it drifted away?
- Are my themes coming through?

We'll look at some of those problems in more detail in a moment, but while you make the beat sheet there is only one you need to think about.

Thumbnail notes... **The scene's purpose**

Each scene should be there for a reason. This might be to explain a character's background, to reveal a discovery, to document a ground-breaking encounter between two characters.

You can't edit successfully until you know what each scene is meant to be doing in the story.

If a scene doesn't have a purpose it shouldn't be in the book.

If the scenes all have purpose, the whole novel will. The story will unfold in the most compelling, persuasive way and you'll have enough contrast and variety to keep the reader entertained.

The beat sheet helps you to clarify what a scene's purpose is. This may have changed since you first thought of the scene, and may not be at all clear in the first draft. If you know the purpose of a scene, you can edit it effectively. If you don't know, you're hacking and twiddling blindly.

How to make your beat sheet

You can write your beat sheet on paper or on a spreadsheet. I prefer paper because I get to do childishly pleasurable things like colouring in, but do whatever suits you. The principles are the same.

Find pens in all the colours of the rainbow. Or take a clutch of more conventional biros and some fluorescent markers – so you can write in red and underline with, say, fluorescent green. I'll explain why in a minute.

Draw a margin on one or other side of the page. It doesn't matter which. This will be for your timeline, which I'll explain properly in a moment. If you're using a spreadsheet, this will be one of your columns.

Now read through the manuscript. Some people prefer a printout; I'm happy to read on screen. If loading the text into Word will tempt you to start editing, then maybe a hard copy is better.

The format might make a difference too. Manuscripts are traditionally printed double spaced, but some writers find it easier to turn on their critical faculties if the page is single spaced, more like a finished work.

As you read, summarise each scene and its intended purpose. Use as few words as possible – the aim is to cram as much onto the page as possible so that you can assess large portions of the novel at a glance.

Here's an example. This is what I put for the opening of my first book in *The Unseen Hand* series.

Amyntas watching, deadly. Charlie goes to shed – wow hi-tech. Mark arrives, finds Charlie dead. Gai on plane, irritated.

If it's a scene that is establishing character I'll put *Gai intro*, but hopefully Gai will be doing something a bit more besides having himself described. Hence *Gai on plane, irritated.*

This is where the coloured pens come in. If Amyntas, Charlie and Mark are one story strand, I'll do them in, say, blue. If Gai is another, he'll be red, or if they're eventually going to have scenes together I'll keep him blue but underline in a pink highlighter, say. Sub-plot material could have another colour.

This way, you can see at a glance if the characters are as prominent as you want, if you drift away from certain people for too long, and if you're bringing threads together.

I started doing this when I was writing a teen adventure series with five main characters, and the publisher wanted to be sure each character had an equal amount of action. So Amyntas, Charlie and Mark may be denoted by just one colour, or they might, if they're going to diverge, each have colours of their own.

Save one colour, though. You need to draw in what you're going to change.

More on that in a moment.

Some rules for the beat sheet

1: Put the scene's *intended* purpose
This may not be how it reads at the moment. Many scenes in a first draft will ramble dementedly. Or end too soon. In this exercise you are not assessing how well you've written the scene already but how you will ultimately use it.

2 Don't worry about how to edit the scene
Leave that for the next task, the actual rewriting. Once you get re-immersed in the story, the 'right' solution will usually arise naturally.

3 Don't try to rewrite right now
Two reasons. One – you will be in the wrong mindset. Second reason – many more things may change and you will probably be wasting your time. You may need to change the order of certain scenes. That's a pain in the

backside if you've already edited them to follow in a sequence. It may even put you off making a change that you know you should make.

4: Include the boring, repetitive and awful
Don't leave the 'dreadful' scenes out of the beat sheet. Put them in. Later on we will deal with restructuring and reordering. Once you see the big picture you might discover you have a good use for your most abominable scene. In a different position it might fill a gap very nicely, or you could add more material to it and really make it sing. But if you don't include it in the beat sheet you won't know it's available to be used.

Scenework is teamwork

A scene must be interesting in its own right but also because of what came before and what comes after it. That's why there's little point in editing one by itself until you know where it fits into the novel as a whole.

Draw emoticons

As well as using colours I also draw little emoticons. A ! for a shock, :0 for peril, ;) for humour, ? for mystery and so on. A curly arrow is useful for plot twists. I also have variations for whether a scene is exciting, touching or frightening.

With these I can see where the emotional ups and downs are, and if the whole book is building in the right way.

Some people I know use coloured stickers or rubber stamps. If you're using spreadsheets, your emoticons will be %s, &s, !!s, *s etc.

I adapt the emoticons for whatever I'm writing. If it's a literary novel I probably won't need many for physical danger, but in a thriller I'll have to find emoticons for each level of danger. (Exclamation marks in multiples do it quite nicely.)

It's also handy to devise a way of showing medium-level disappointment compared with utter disaster.

By the end, you should have a rather colourful document with drawings all over it that doesn't look like a piece of work. But it is your bible for how you will finally shape your manuscript.

You will diagnose from it where to swap things around, where to write more about a particular character, where you can cut, where you should turn up the drama and where you need to lighten the mood. You can tell if your danger peaks too early and if the story runs out of steam.

Keep it brief

The beat sheet is an 'at-a-glance' document. It works best if you get it into as small a space as possible – hence the extremely condensed writing style. I find I can get a 50,000-word teen thriller onto one sheet of A4, in small writing.

With more intricate novels, though, that's not possible. The beat sheet for *My Memories of a Future Life* ran to nine pages, and the novel was so complex to rewrite that I had multiple layers of Post-it notes all over it too. But it wrested order out of a giant, sagging monster. And for many months it was the most precious document in my house.

Timeline

The margin you left is for the timeline.

Whenever you come across an element of the story that has to take place on a certain day, for instance Christmas 1987, write it alongside the action.

Also write in if a deadline has appeared – such as *two hours before the air runs out*. There will be some blanks, but that doesn't matter. Write down the timings you do have, against the plot, so that you build up a calendar of the story.

Then, when you revise the passage where you blithely wrote *last week*, you will know exactly what it should say.

If your plot includes a race against the clock, the timing often needs to be worked out to the minute. With the beat sheet it's simplicity itself to write the timings down against the plot events and make sure it all works.

Task 8½ Making changes

Remember the colour you reserved? Use this to draw in where you're going to reorder, repurpose, expand or excise.

You may have to add scenes, or push them to more dramatic conclusions. This can all easily be seen and written in in your correction colour.

Here's a bit more about the problems you are looking for and how to decide what to do about them.

Thumbnail notes... Pace

The pace of a scene is how swiftly or slowly it plays. This depends not just on how that scene is written but also on the other scenes around it. A scene may seem slow if it comes after action, but it may be faster than some other scenes. So pace is judged in relation to the pace of other scenes around it.

If you've had several fast scenes with plenty of revelations, you might want a slower one so that the reader can catch their breath. You may think that if your book proceeds at breakneck speed from start to finish that makes it a rollercoaster read. It may be, but it may just as easily leave the reader punch drunk. Even in the most dynamic thriller there will be quiet moments – a calm before another storm.

The term pace is also used to apply to the novel as a whole. It's usual for the story to gather momentum towards the end. This heightens the sense of drama. So the scenes much earlier in the book may have to be more leisurely.

Check if the pace of your novel varies enough – or too much. And if it builds to a suitable crescendo.

Thumbnail notes… **Mood**

Like pace, the mood needs to vary. If you have a tragic revelation you may want to precede it with a scene that is lighter in mood, and then the two gain from the contrast of being next to each other.

However, it's easy to get carried away with juxtapositions of mood. A flip from tragedy to lighthearted can work very well but it can also look too abrupt, as though the scenes come from separate novels. It's a hard thing to judge, because you want contrast but you also want consistency.

In this example, the obvious solution is to tone either the comedy or tragedy down – perhaps to turn the tragic revelation into a painful mishap.

Check on the beat sheet whether the mood of the novel varies enough – or if it borders on schizophrenia.

Thumbnail notes… **Classic story structure**

Another way that Hollywood scriptwriters use beat sheets is to check that the major changes in direction come in the right places. (Remember the three-act structure I mentioned when we were building the basic story?) In films, these 'changes' are usually a quarter of the way through, half-way through, and three-quarters through.

That might not be your style, of course, and may not be appropriate for the genre you are writing. But if you are writing a genre that is strong on plot, you might be reassured if you find your novel splits into acts in this way.

Alternatively, you may feel that the story is uneven, or there is a dull bit in the middle. Doing this simple division into thirds may suggest where the problem lies. Fixing it may be as simple as shuffling a few scenes into new positions.

Thumbnail notes... Character arcs

If characters have taken matters into their own hands, it is helpful to check out their progression through the story. This is their arc, or the way they evolve. Your main characters should have a satisfying beginning, middle and end. A lot of this will have been covered when you did the detailed synopsis, but it does no harm to check again whether their role is satisfying and plausible. Sometimes the beat sheet reveals that your main character does very little. Or that their story disappears half-way through and that they are watching on the sidelines while somebody else solves the problems, has the challenges and develops. It's easy to do, so watch out for it.

Check, also, that at the end, the main character has been through the most significant change in the story. That's one of the things that makes them the main character.

You can check this on a straightforward list. Or if you prefer more visual imagery, try the graphs or music staves approach that you first played with when assessing your synopsis in section 1 (p71).

Thumbnail notes... Beginnings

In your first draft, you probably plunged in and told the story where you felt like starting it. Now is the time to think critically about whether you've started in the right place.

Some writers take a while to warm up. They find they don't really get into their stride until the fourth or fifth chapter.

Try this – read your novel from chapter 3, imagining that is the beginning. What situation are your characters in? Is it more interesting and intriguing? Could you slot in the background as you go so that the reader can understand it?

Other writers try too hard for the drama and start the story too late in the action. If you find you've had to include a lot of background detail that doesn't easily fit into the action, perhaps you need to make those chapters into more straightforward narrative and start the story a little earlier.

It could even be that your beginning – dramatic as it is – should be the culmination of all the events. In fact, it should be the end!

Also check that your beginning sets up the end. For instance, my novel *My Memories of a Future Life* opened with a concert pianist struck down by a mysterious injury that stopped her playing.

The end, therefore, would have to resolve this question in some way – because readers will always attach a lot of importance to the first questions they come across.

Something still wrong?

If you feel the novel still doesn't gel into a coherent whole, here are some rescue remedies.

Remedy 1: Start at the end
If you start assessing the novel at the end you can see if the scenes all point in the direction you want them to. Or if there are bits missing, or parts that are too flabby.

Visual artists often do a similar thing. If they're drawing an object they are familiar with, they draw it upside down. Either they translate it in their heads into an upside-down picture, or they turn the object itself upside down and sketch what they see. The purpose is the same – to see the detail and the shape afresh.

This is what happens if you assess the book as an end point and assemble it backwards. Suddenly you will see where you need to write more, and what is clogging the story up.

Remedy 2: Write a mission statement

If the novel still feels like a great buzzing muddle, step back further. Write a few paragraphs that state

- what you intend the audience to feel about the characters
- the experience you want them to get from the story
- which scenes should ideally be powerful and the effect you want them to have.

This may take some time. Summarising the goals of a big sprawling manuscript is not easy.

It might help to imagine you are writing a blurb or a review and that you have understood everything the writer was trying to do. Be specific about the story, the themes and the mood. *Two brothers struggle to overcome the shadow of their Mafia past, and end up fighting their own family. The results are heartbreaking.*

Once you have written this statement you will be able to judge the purpose of each scene – and what you should do with it.

A mission statement can also help you discover some flaws. You might write *this is the story of two friends who fall out irrevocably,* and realise that although you start with this intention, the two characters all but disappear in the second half.

Conversely, you might realise that although you started out with that aim, some other characters took over. So maybe you should beef up their role earlier on and downplay the two friends.

You might also find there are threads you have set in motion and abandoned. There may be a lot you can do with those.

Once you have written your mission statement, do another beat sheet. You should now be able to tell what the purpose of each scene is, where the pace and mood are going wrong, what to keep and what to cut, and what you should add.

If you decide to completely restructure

Some restructuring is inevitable. Most of it can be evaluated on the beat sheet. But if you decide to make major alterations and put an event at the beginning that was previously at the end, the consequences may be too complex to evaluate on the beat sheet. The same goes for if you decide to introduce a different major development.

If you're going to do that, go back to the cards stage. Write a completely new set of cards for the book, using the first draft, and slot in the new ramifications to check how the development pans out. Once you've played with that, write some new rough scenes, then paste a new version together. Remember to keep the old one just in case.

Don't try to edit it yet – leave it as a rough cut. Then write another beat sheet to plan how to tackle the fine editing stage.

Assessing an abandoned manuscript.

You can use the beat sheet to assess an abandoned manuscript, provided it is finished and you don't plan on adding a lot of new material. If you never got to the end, or if you think you'll need to develop the story or characters more, you're probably better to use the cards. That way you can explore consequences from the scenario and see what hidden story emerges. If you want a more refreshed perspective, assess the story using the rescue remedies.

Some dos and don'ts

- Do read the manuscript fast and not too closely. At the moment what you're looking at is the structure, development, the contrast of one scene with another, the mood.

- Do not look at the writing, the pace, the characterisation, the repetition (how everyone seems to be wearing orange baseball caps... in one of my novels I didn't realise that whenever a rope appeared it was blue).
- Don't be disheartened if you discover a significant problem. You've just made an extremely important diagnosis. Congratulate yourself on a job well done.

Inevitably you'll have some other sundry ideas for the rewriting that don't fit into the beat sheet format (extra scenes, too many blue ropes...). Note these separately, with page numbers, so that as you revise, you can tick them off.

Why the beat sheet is different from the cards game

The cards game allows you to test the structural soundness of set-up, event and consequence. The beat sheet tests fitness for purpose – whether a scene works, what the purpose should be and how it should be rewritten.

One is a tool for generating a story. The other helps you assess the story after you have written it.

Aims recap for the rewrite plan

What are you trying to get right at this stage?
You are aiming to create a set of instructions that tell you
how to fine-edit each scene, so it does the best job for
the whole novel.

What are you ignoring for now?
You are ignoring the details – again. The beat sheet is
another top-down exercise. You are treating your
manuscript as a rough to be pulled about, chopped, recut
and manipulated. So no fretting over your wonky
phrasing. Save that for … tomorrow.

5 The rewrites

You've written a manuscript. It's rough, but you've got exciting plans for it.

This is where you make every scene a finely honed piece of storytelling. Where you feel the true novel emerge. Not perhaps the book you first envisioned, but who could know how it would turn out when you first started playing with it? But now you've tested the story and the characters. You can produce a novel you'll be proud to show to others. This is where the writing turns into a labour of love. From now on, it's the home stretch.

Aims

What are you trying to get right at this stage?
See below.

What are you ignoring?
Nothing. There's no leaving anything until later. There is no later.

This is where you bring it all together. But your beat sheet will make it an efficient, manageable task. When you come across problems they will be small scale because you've already solved the bigger ones. You shouldn't find yourself wondering what on earth to do with a scene, because that brain-work has been done already.

And yes, you finally have permission to blitz the typos.

Task 9 Revising your manuscript

Have you made these creative decisions yet?
Before you start, there are three creative decisions you need to make, if you haven't made them already. They will affect the way you present your story and characters.

1: Viewpoint

Think about the viewpoint you'll use for the novel.

*Thumbnail notes...*Viewpoint

The viewpoint is the character whose eyes the story is seen through. For instance, a first-person narrative is the story of someone who the story is happening to, told by them.

The choice of viewpoint imposes logical constraints. In first person, you can't easily show many things that happen when that character isn't there. But this may not matter – or it may even make the story more powerful.

The other common viewpoint is third person. With third person you have a lot more freedom, but not total carte blanche. There are still logical constraints. Third-person viewpoint is rarely that of 'all the people in the entire world'. It is 'the experiences of the main characters you are writing about'. You still have to beware of stepping outside that to give new information that these characters couldn't naturally have encountered.

Writers using third person might be tempted to drift into the point of view of a minor character to shoehorn in a piece of information that would be difficult to explain otherwise. This is a logical cheat – and it can be dislocating for the reader. But in some genres it is accepted – eg thrillers. So check your working library to see what published writers can get away with in your genre.

The logical constraints of viewpoint may also be bent if you use a commenting narrative voice. More on this in a moment.

2: Your novel's format

What format will you tell the story in? You don't have to stick to straightforward, chronological prose.

Thumbnail notes...Story format

Stories can be told in a number of formats. Chapters may alternate between different narrators, or between past and present. You might decide to present the whole novel as a series of letters, or a diary, or emails. Or newspaper columns, as if you were writing the character's adventures in a Sunday magazine.

3: Your novel's tone or voice

You will also need to establish the overall tone of the writing. This may be a no-brainer – you've got a natural writing voice and that's all there is to it.

Some authors use a voice that is different from their natural writing voice. Especially if they're pitching at a particular genre, such as young adult or thrillers. If it's your first venture into one of these it's worth trying out a few voices to see what comes most naturally to you.

Another decision you must make consciously is whether your narrative voice is going to comment on the action or not.

Thumbnail notes...Narrative voice, or tone

Narrative tone is the way the story is told. It's the tone in the writer's voice – which is why the terms 'voice' and 'tone' tend to be interchanged.

It is often heavily tied to the genre of the story as it sets the world of the novel. So it may be a frothy world, or a dark and dangerous one. It may be comic or tragic. Slapstick – or sensitive and perceptive.

It can be anything you like – but it should be consistent. Whatever the ups and downs of the plot, the writer's voice should have a distinct – and consistent – way to tell them. So a tragedy can happen in a frothy world, and comedy in a dark one. Tone is not about what events you can include, but how you tell them. Again, the best way to learn is to consult your working library.

Another important aspect of the narrative voice is whether it comments. Some narrators tell the story exactly at face value. Others will use their description of a scene to direct the reader to think a certain way (to find it funny, perhaps, or despicable).

Generally, if you decide your narrator will be the commenting type, they should comment most of the way through the story. If you tell most of the story at face value and slip in a sudden nudge and wink, it destroys the reader's sense of immersion in the story. It's like putting a laugh track on a story that didn't have one before.

Intruding commentary is not just confined to moments of comedy. Writers often use commentary to let us know who the bad guy is. This is fine – if the other characters are presented with commentary too. But don't let us make up our own mind about some characters and not others. This change in tone from subtlety to spoonfeeding is irritating. Because readers who enjoy subtle characterization usually do not want to be told what to think.

Commentary can be very useful, though. If you comment you might be able to slip in the viewpoints of characters who aren't as prominent as the main characters, sidestepping the constraints of your viewpoint.

The key to a good narrative tone is to be consistent. If you wish to comment, do so by all means. If you wish to leave the reader alone to make up their own mind, then do so.

But you can't usually get away with both.

Establishing a narrative voice isn't so pressing as establishing a viewpoint because it doesn't present many logistical problems.

Many writers find a natural tone evolves as they get immersed. Unevennesses are relatively easy to fix on another read-through.

How to use the beat sheet

Obviously you are going to use the beat sheet as a guide to the scene's purpose. It might be to introduce the irritated Gai, to show Jenny confronting her flatmate, to increase the tension between a pair who will become lovers.

Also, take notice of the emoticons.

This is where you can tell not only what emotion you must squeeze out of a scene, but how much. Check whether you wrote a single exclamation mark, no exclamation mark – or a triple.

Remember that a scene's impact depends on the scenes around it and what has built up to it. There's no point in writing all the scenes so that they bellow at the tops of their voices. Look at the emoticons to see whether you're meant to have worked up to bellowing pitch, or whether it would be more appropriate merely to clear your throat.

Take your time

The rewrites stage can't be hurried, even though you are thoroughly prepared for it. Expect it to take at least as long as writing the first draft.

You may have noticed that I call this the rewrites stage. Plural. Here's why.

You won't be able to do everything you need to in a scene on the first pass. To get the dialogue really sharp you need to be thinking in a certain way – some writers like to read it out loud.

Physical descriptions require another type of mind-set. If you're fine-tuning some comedy you may need a separate pass to do that too.

To pull all that together and create the desired mood for the scene may take yet another pass. Yet another, perhaps, to add that all-important touch that makes it entertaining and keeps the audience's attention.

Thumbnail notes... **Making a scene entertaining**

Always try to make the outcome of the scene a little surprising. Ideally, the reader should not be able to predict from the beginning of the scene how it turns out at the end. But this doesn't always have to be a big surprise. A tiny twist will do.

You can probably see from this that rewriting each scene will require, on average, five separate critical faculties, which you probably can't keep running in your head all at once. That means you'll have to go through each scene an average of five times.

Some writers prefer to do a different sort of editing each day. Perhaps they zip through a few scenes and tackle the dialogue at one sitting, then go back over it for tone, beautifying descriptions and so on.

You may also have to experiment with a number of approaches before you're satisfied with a scene.

You will write a lot, and then cut most of it out. This is normal. So for the rewrites you have to develop a strong critical sense and a streak of ruthlessness.

Your Outtakes file will be one of your best friends.

If you get stuck

You shouldn't get blocked, but you will have minor hiccups. Mostly what will trip you up is deciding how to make a scene interesting while fulfilling its function. If you start to panic, or get stuck, revisit some of the Block busters in section 2 – particularly What comes next (p95), Reincorporation (p92) and Conflict (p92). They can free your creativity just as effectively at this stage as they did earlier.

Don't forget the Outtakes file

You will be making a lot of trips to the Outtakes file, and it will probably become at least half as long as the completed manuscript. How much should you keep?

I try to keep as much as possible. Especially the total rubbish from the first draft, where I was feeling my way with a scene. Raw though it is, sometimes there is a freshness in the phrasing that's worth preserving. Sometimes when I've finished a scene, I scan through the early version in Outtakes to see if there is a mad flight of words that should be in the final version.

Targets

A word about wordcounts. I love them at the first draft stage, because I want to throw the thing together as fast as possible and be reassured that what I'm creating is big enough to be a novel. But at the rewrite stage, checking the wordcount won't give the same spur, especially if you are cutting and chopping every day.

Personally I don't need targets to keep me revising. The beat sheet usually gets me so excited about what I can do with the story that I don't need to watch my scores to keep myself at the desk.

Some people do set themselves targets – for instance, to revise 5,000 words a week. Or they clipboard off completed revisions into a new file and watch as it grows.

You could also track your progress through the Outtakes file, congratulating yourself as it gets bigger and bigger.

Rewriting the beginning: start as you mean to go on

You know what events you are going to start with and how you are going to slot in the information that will allow the reader to understand them. You also know that the beginning must grab the reader's attention. But when you're polishing the beginning, check that its tone is a true reflection of the novel in its entirety.

Don't write it to be punchy and full of action if you want to take the rest of the book at an amble. Quite a lot of novice writers do this – they race out of the starting gates like a greased greyhound and then meander into a long reflection on the significance of fly fishing. This will undoubtedly impress for the first few pages – and then be very disappointing, if not baffling.

You certainly do need a beginning that grabs attention. But make sure the way you do it is in harmony with the book as a whole.

Grabbing attention does not have to be done at full throttle. You can intrigue, or present a fascinating dilemma, or a character full of beguiling contradictions.

Make your dialogue sing – in different voices

You might find that all your characters sound essentially the same. An easy way to develop a consistent, distinctive style for a character is to copy off their dialogue to another file and look at it in isolation. This is especially useful if you want their speech rhythms or habits to be a little different from your 'normal' speaking voice.

Although do beware of 'doing accents'. Sure, they are distinctive, but funny spellings that are hard for the reader to 'hear' in their head can quickly become wearing, as can adopting a style that you cannot mimick naturally. Only do this if you really are good at it.

In any case, verbal tics are not characterisation.

Thumbnail notes... **Giving characters distinct voices**
Characters need to be individuals. Some writers attempt to do this by giving them distinctive costumes or maybe vocal tics. Very often it isn't satisfying because the reader can tell that is all on the surface. The distinctiveness must come from what is in the characters' hearts. What comes across in good dialogue is different views and motivations, different things that people want.

Other alerts for smart revision

Each time you come across the following, make your critical radar ping:

- Any facts
- Physical descriptions
- Story consistency
- Darlings, or special pieces of writing you don't want to delete
- Telling, not showing
- Any new scene start-up
- Irrelevant relics of your previous draft
- Consistency in narrative tone
- Timings

1: Facts – and checking them

You'll have done a lot of this at the research phase, but while you were writing you probably came across new gaps in your knowledge and flung a statement in willy-nilly.

Now, as you go through the manuscript in detail, keep an eye out for any facts you have fudged and check them.

Readers expect facts to be just that, not what you've made up, in much the same as they expect you to use grammar and spelling properly.

If you include something and the reader spots it is wrong, it can undermine the credibility of the whole book.

2: Descriptions

Check descriptions for consistency. Everything from characters' hair colour, disabilities, likes and dislikes; or the colour of the carpet in the duke's palace. It's amazing how easy it is to get the details of your own world wrong.

Like you did in the first draft, keep separate files for this. If you modify anything, make a note. Do this for character histories too.

3: Story strands

Most novels have a main plot and a sub-plot, and if you're trying to do anything fancy with flashbacks that adds an extra complication. You need to keep control of them and how you're developing them.

If they are complex, I start another work file for each and as I finalise a section, I copy them in.

In *My Memories of a Future Life* it was important that the main character came to realise certain things about her early life. So I had one file in which I kept track of all these revelations. Another file contained just the scenes involving the sub-plot. Not only could I could check they were consistent, I could also make sure they always escalated.

As with physical descriptions and character histories, it is much easier to check these details if they are distilled into one file than to haphazardly search through the entire manuscript.

4: Telling, not showing

A lot of the editing you are doing is to make the scene slicker and faster. There will probably be a lot of fluff where you were feeling your way, or making up a description of a room for the first time.

Certainly fluff has to go. But don't get into the summarising frame of mind. Don't forget to show instead of tell (for a quick reminder, see p81).

Also don't become so fixated on the purpose of a scene that you strip away too much. It's beyond the scope of this book to offer detailed descriptions of how a scene works, and your favoured textbooks no doubt cover this, but it's probably useful to think of it this way.

*Thumbnail notes...*Letting scenes develop

Look at the purpose of a scene and ask yourself how that is going to become clear. Usually the purpose won't be clear at the beginning, it will have developed by the end. Now write it at a pace that makes that development look natural.

When stripping out the fluff, don't forget to allow the scene time to evolve naturally out of what the characters say and do.

Sounds contradictory, doesn't it? It's a matter of judgement and practice. As in the first draft phase, if you suspect you are rushing, take a break and read something else to get you back into the mood.

5: New scene start-up: does the reader have all the information they need?

Not all the work you do on this draft will be pruning. You may have to add some basic information to make sure the reader understands what is going on in each scene.

It is extraordinarily easy to forget to do this. In the thick of writing, you know what is going on. But the reader will not necessarily.

Here's a checklist of information you may need to add.

At the start of a scene Where the characters are, who's present and what they're doing. Stage directions, in fact.

When starting a new chapter Stage directions are particularly important with chapter beginnings, as the reader will expect there to be some kind of break in the narrative. (They may even have taken a break themselves as it's a natural point to put the book down.)

Make sure you have said
- when the scene takes place (*some days later* or *it wasn't until Thursday that Mary got a chance to visit the bar again*)
- where it is (*Clive's bar was under a solicitor's office on the main street*).

Other information you may have to give your reader, so that they understand what's going on:

- Factual information – disguised as natural dialogue and action, not as exposition (where characters or the narrator stop everything to explain the plot, or how a fridge works)
- Groundwork for plot crises and other developments – set up with sufficient, but subtle warnings.

These details may seem obvious but they are very important to make sure your reader doesn't get confused.

6: Kill your darlings

A word of warning about phrases or passages you particularly like. Ask yourself, do they really fit?

All writers are in danger of spoiling a novel with indulgent bits. Nothing should stay in the story if it doesn't belong there, but writers aren't perfect. Our hearts often override our critical instincts. We often cling to things we shouldn't.

That's the meaning of the phrase Kill your darlings.

A darling might be something as small as a poetic description, or as significant as a plot strand. But something's wrong. Perhaps it's a bit irrelevant. Perhaps it interrupts the pace or the flow, or is wrong for the tone. Perhaps it's from an earlier version and fitted very well then, but doesn't now.

You like it but at the same time you know, deep down, that it doesn't fit.

If you simply cannot do the deletion thing, ask yourself why. Is it:

- a piece of research you particularly wanted to get in
- an anecdote you want to use, perhaps because it was true or for some other personal reason
- a character or situation, for personal reasons as above
- a description, which, although adorable, repeats material you already have
- a passage of writing you simply love and don't want to bin.

If the answer to any of these questions is yes, you may well be harbouring a darling. The only reason you're keeping it is because you like it.

This is another reason why you have an Outtakes file. So the darlings can be removed, temporarily, and you can see how the scene goes without it. The darling isn't lost, it's still available if you really want it. Put it on your website. Or save it for a future novel.

More seriously, there is a practical reason for keeping darlings. You might genuinely have a use for it elsewhere in this novel. If you need another scene with those elements you can use the darling as the basis.

7: Relics of your previous draft
As your novel evolves, so will your intentions for character or plot strands. What worked in a previous

version of the story won't necessarily work in this one. It might be irrelevant or too complicating.

Now you are more sure of your characters and your story, you need to be on the lookout for moments like this and take them out.

8: Narrative tone
This can go awry very easily in the race to get everything else right, but it's one of the biggest ways to derail the reader. Always check if your narrative tone is consistent (Thumbnail note, p137).

9: Timeline
Whenever there's a reference to time, check it against the timeline on the beat sheet. (See how easy it is?)

Keep the beat sheet too, even when you've finished. If later on you are fortunate enough to get your book in front of an editor, these niggly points of consistency are something they will want you to check.

The usual way to do it is to read the manuscript, writing down every reference to time. This might not be too onerous, but if your plot relies on split-second timing it could be torture as you try to remember whether you did, in fact, plan it rigorously and therefore whether your story is robust. You will be very grateful you made the timing watertight at this stage, and that you made a record to prove it.

Spelling and other stuff

At last you can tidy up the spelling, grammar and punctuation.

If this is fills you with dismay rather than relief, you're not alone in this. Some prominent published writers have immense trouble with these trifling details.

But trivial as they are, bad spelling, grammar and punctuation interfere with the experience of a novel and can be enough to put off a publisher or agent.

If you can't see the mistakes yourself, it is well worth bribing a friend or family member to take a look. Or there are many excellent books on the market that will explain the basics.

Chapters

You might want to split the book into its chapters and sections as you go, or you might find it easier to do it once you're largely happy with the draft.

But do try to make sure that chapters end on a suspenseful or intriguing note, pulling the reader along to the next one, while still seeming complete. Often I find that if a chapter is a little too long and I want to split it in two, some tweaking is required to make the chapter ending feel right.

Stick to your plan... but change if you must

The beat sheet is your map through a labyrinth of words.

But a new inspiration can strike at any time, especially with a story you've been brewing for this long. You might think you've finished worrying about the plot or the structure, but some little creative vandal didn't realise it was home time and suddenly bowls an idea in.

Embrace it. And – don't tear up the plan.

Be professional. Assess the change thoroughly and rigorously by going to the beat sheet. Evaluate the effects it will have. Weigh up the pros and cons of doing it – with the cards game if you have to. It may be the best idea since Bridget Jones started her diary, in which case that should be obvious.

Scribble the changes on the beat sheet and then carry on.

But don't abandon your beat sheet. It is crucial to making sure you write this book as well as you possibly can and bring out its potential. If you abandon it, pretty soon you won't know where you're going.

Finished: are you sure?

While you should have done a lot of improving by the time you reach the end of this draft, it's always advisable to put it aside again for a while and then reread it.

The second draft isn't the absolute final draft, but it should be pretty close. Be prepared to do a little troubleshooting afterwards – what builders call snagging. Don't be surprised if you still find some points you want to tweak. However, any rewrites at this stage should be much swifter than they were before.

If, each time you reread, you get an inkling that something is amiss, listen to that critical voice. The chances are that something is still slightly off.

Aims recap for Task 9

What are you trying to get right at this stage?
Everything. This is where you make the novel as good as you possibly can.

What are you ignoring for now?
Nothing, I'm afraid. If you get a niggle that something is wrong, you take it very seriously indeed.

Keep your Outtakes file, your synopses and your beat sheet

When you've finally finished, don't bin your Outtakes file. Novels go through many revisions, even once a publisher has taken them on. (Don't be shy. Most people who start a novel are aiming for this.) You may find that what you have so painfully removed actually does have a place – perhaps at a different point in the story, or edited and disbursed throughout the text.

But don't use this as a reason not to do as thorough a job on the writing as you can.

The beat sheet might also be useful. Not just for the timeline, as mentioned earlier, but if you need to quickly reacquaint yourself with your novel before meeting an editor or agent. Often by the time they read your novel and want to talk about it, you have forgotten most of it while they could answer an A-level paper.

Keep the synopsis documents. They are also gold dust, even though the story may have evolved a long way from them. I'll tell you why in the next section.

You can probably get rid of the cards, though. I've never found a use for them beyond the phase in which they are actually needed.

6 Sending your novel to seek its fortune

The publishing business
You presumably are writing in the hope of making a sale to a publisher.

Competition among first-time novelists is tougher than ever. Agents and publishers are drowning in manuscripts that are 'mostly good' but not of a professional standard. Although they are looking for literary gold, they are also looking for the first excuse to say no and move onto the next script.

You need to give your novel the best chance to impress them. But many first-time novelists send out their work before it has been sufficiently polished. Do not – repeat DO NOT – let the novel out of your sight until you have fixed everything you possibly can.

Don't send it off because you're exhausted with the whole process. Or because your family and friends are nagging you to. They may believe you only have to push it through a publisher's letterbox for the Harry Potter machine to soar into action.

They couldn't be more wrong. Unless you're famous or infamous, your manuscript will have to work extremely hard and be incredibly lucky to get a break.

However, new writers are published all the time, by publishers big and small.

So take your time and fix any problems. Even if it takes you another month or two, that is much better than blowing your chance to have the novel taken seriously.

There are writers who polish the same manuscript ad infinitum, year after year, and never seem prepared to let it go.

You don't want to do that either.

Getting feedback

This is the stage where an outsider's opinion might help you iron out the glitches you can't see for yourself – and there are always a few. By the same token, though, there may not be nearly as many as you think.

Who should you show it to?

Friends and family
Your friends and family are probably deeply intrigued about what you've been up to and asking when they're going to get a look.

They may not be your most useful critics, though. Most people's nearest and dearest don't think in a critical way. They're so impressed that you have produced anything at all that they say it's wonderful because they don't want to discourage you. Or they might be jealous of what you've accomplished and give you only grudging praise when you deserve much more – it all depends on the politics in your family.

Or they just want you to get the darn thing out of the door, see above.

You're not even safe showing the book to friends who have no axe to grind. One friend of mine rhapsodised about how much he'd enjoyed my first ghosted novel, a teen gothic romance called *Mirror Image*. He was, like me, an English literature graduate so I basked proudly.

Until he said: 'You put HER in it, didn't you?' He then quoted my description of the girl who caused the story's mischief.

I realised who he meant. Someone we both knew from college. Physically she was a little like the girl in my book. But I hadn't put her in the book at all. The physical description was inspired totally by the cover, which the publisher had already designed. I made the character look like that because it annoyed me when covers weren't consistent with what was inside the book.

Now it dawned on me that the sole reason my friend had enjoyed the book was because he thought I'd been writing about HER. No other reason.

So your friends, bless them, will latch onto the oddest things in your novel.

However, they can give you useful feedback if you brief them properly.

Ask them to annotate the manuscript as they read. Not to correct your spellings or grammar (unless you're having trouble with them). You don't want them to solve any problems, either – just point out where they were enjoying the book and where they weren't.

You want them to highlight
- boring parts – mark them *zzz*
- hard-to-understand parts – mark those *???*
- parts they liked – mark with a tick

- stretches of credibility – mark these *Noooo!!!*

Although it can bolster your confidence to know that someone has genuinely enjoyed your book, confidence is not enough in today's market. Even your friends with English degrees are not judging your novel against the standards used by professionals looking for genuinely saleable work.

Other writers
If you have a friend who's a writer, they might be able to give you some helpful pointers. Although this can be a double-edged sword – they might tell you how *they* would write it, not how *you* should. If they don't click with your genre or style they may end up giving you mistaken advice – what's conventional in one genre might be totally unbearable in another.

Writers' groups can be a useful way to get support and feedback, although much depends on the group dynamics. Before reading your work out, go to a few sessions and suss out the individual personalities and the way they give criticism.

Some people's tastes may not be right for the genre you write; or their motives for criticising may not be honest and transparent. Or they may be well-meaning but clueless. Decide whose advice you would find useful to improve your novel, so that when you read your work out, you know who to take notice of.

Professional critique services and tutors

These days a lot of first-time novelists get a professional critical MOT before submitting to publishers and agents. This could be from a course or a critiquing service. As with writers' groups, do some research first. Look for testimonials, obviously. And make sure you will get personalised feedback on your novel's strengths and weaknesses – from someone who is suitable to comment on that genre.

How to use criticism positively

Getting serious constructive criticism can be quite harrowing. You may feel very exposed when you let someone read your fiction for the first time, especially a stranger. No matter how nicely they put their suggestions, it can feel very wounding.

Creative writing courses often include advice on how to take criticism, so a word about it here.

It is not criticism of you, it is criticism of the novel. They are two separate things, although it may not feel like that by this stage. You have probably put your feelings, your fantasies and your fears into this work, like nothing else you have ever done before. You may have included events that happened to you and what you think of other people. Intimate experiences and painful memories.

The professional critic is not criticising any of this, or what the novel reveals about you. They don't take any notice of that, in fact. They are diagnosing what's right and wrong with your novel, not what is good or bad about you.

Writers' groups and courses may give their criticisms in front of other writers, which can feel quite exposing until you are used to it. So for your first novel you may prefer the less public experience of a written report from a consultancy.

Sending it out

Agent or publisher?

Most fiction publishers these days prefer to receive submissions from agents rather than directly from writers.

Almost every serious writer has a copy of *Writers' and Artists' Yearbook*, which lists all the UK agents and publishers, and guidelines on how to approach them. You can usually find this on line too. Some will want a completed manuscript and synopsis, some will ask for the first 50 pages only. Some will ask that you phone or email first to discuss the project.

Whatever they ask for, do it. Don't just send them your novel anyway; they have these procedures for a reason.

And take notice of the genres they handle. If they say 'no science fiction', they've said it because they mean it. Your space opera isn't going to change their mind.

Task 10 Your submission package

Writers' and Artists' Yearbook also gives excellent advice on making an approach that looks professional and will be taken seriously. But generally your submission package needs to consist of three elements

- A cover letter
- A synopsis
- The manuscript or manuscript excerpt

It's easier to write the synopsis before the letter, so I'll deal with that first.

The synopsis

Your synopsis is a summary of what happens in the novel. It is one of the most important selling documents you'll write for your manuscript.

Most writers hate writing synopses. I've been a journalist, used to filleting and précising, picking out the important points in a document and making a condensed whole out of them. And I still find writing a synopsis is agony.

First let's examine just what makes it so disagreeable. Then we know what we're dealing with.

- When you strip a story down to its bare events, it looks soulless. It doesn't encapsulate the experience of the book. A synopsis describes the

events but the novel is so much more than just what happens.
- Squeezing 100,000 words into a side of A4 – or maybe two – is ridiculous.
- It will spoil your plot twists. If someone reads them in the synopsis they will get them devoid of atmosphere and impact. They won't share what they mean to the characters. The agent/publisher then won't read the novel because it will have been spoiled.
- What about all these good bits you can't fit in?

If it's any comfort, some agents don't like synopses either. They look at them only so that they can see the writer has an idea of where they are going, and as guidance in case they get lost in the manuscript themselves.

So fear not, your novel will not always be judged solely by the outline you write of its events. But write it you must, for it proves you are professional and have done the process properly. And for every agent or publisher who doesn't want a synopsis, there's another who does.

Let's grit our teeth and do it.

How to write the darned thing

The moan above does give us some useful action points.
- Just listing the events isn't enough. You need to encapsulate the experience of the book.

- The synopsis needs to read well, as it will probably be the first lengthy document the publisher/agent sees from you.
- Expect that it will take time to hone and polish.

This is one of the writing jobs that you will never manage if you try to do it right all in one go. So we take it in stages.

1:Summarise the story events

If you have kept your original synopsis, you may be able to use this as a starting point. Just go through and alter what's changed. Or write it from your beat sheet. And be grateful for the amount of work I've saved you.

Otherwise, you'll need to go through the manuscript.

Start by summarizing the main points in each chapter. This will probably be far too long and a dull read. But it will show you what the key plot points are.

2: Make them into a mini-story

Once you have the main points you have to make them into a mini-story of their own.

At this point, you will need to start pruning. Read the mini-story and see if it would still make sense if minor events were dropped. Do the same for minor characters. Ideally you should include only the central characters and you might find you can shrink your cast to just one main character or group.

3: Tell, not show

Yes, you read that right. Tell the reader why the events that happen to these people are important. Your events list might say *Karl goes hang-gliding, bungee jumping and decides to live as a woman.* Now tell us why. *Karl, at the age of 32, is told he has only six months to live. He decides he's going to do all the things that scare him or that he's never done before. He goes...*

Notice how summarised this is. In your manuscript you probably took ages showing how Karl felt and so on, but in your synopsis you can't wait for the reader's intelligence join the dots. *James is fascinated by new neighbour "Karla's" kooky energy...*

In your synopsis you summarise, explain and spoonfeed. That's how you squeeze the experience of the book into a small space.

4: Significant, captivating and compelling

- For every event you show, make clear its *significance* in the overall emotional arc of the story.
- Make the plot *captivating* and show it knows where it is going.
- Make your (abbreviated) characters believable and the situations *compelling*.

Show the emotional beats and spell them out so that prospective readers can see the characters go on a journey.

Pace it so it sounds exciting. Use shorter sentences towards the end so that the pace builds. And write it in the present tense – not only is this convention for synopses anyway, it sounds more dynamic.

(In fact here's where writing the synopsis, like the beat sheet, can expose weak points you hadn't thought of. Still, better to find out now...)

On the positive side...

You should also find that your overview reveals themes and resonances you weren't aware of when you were up close to the detail. Make a note of them. They may be useful when writing your covering letter, or even when talking about the novel (which I find in itself an arduous process – first I don't know where to start and when I get into my stride I don't know where to stop).

This whole exercise gets you used to 'talking' about your book to the outside world, which you will have to do when you come to sell it.

Reveal the end or not?

How far do you have to go? If you reveal all the twists you'll leave your audience nothing to discover.

Opinions are divided on this. Some say it is permissible to leave out the ending and to finish on the crucial question of the climax – *Is James about to find out after all? What is the big secret Karl is keeping from him?*

Other writers feel that looks amateurish. Personally, I favour the more professional impression. Editors and agents will have the sense to stop reading the synopsis if they feel it will 'spoil' it all anyway. So do the job properly and tell the story all the way to the end.

Finished? Not quite

Once you've written your synopsis, you have a few more bits of summarizing to do. At some stage you will need some much shorter pitches for your book – yes even shorter. You need a shortened synopsis – a paragraph or two, and a one-sentence pitch.

We are now talking extreme summary.

How to do extreme summary

You need a summary for your cover letter. Preferably a sentence or two. Your novel is probably 100,000 words long and you have to distil it to 50 or so. That's a problem of biblical dimensions. What do you include? What do you leave out? How do you do justice to it?

The easiest way to do it is to study the blurbs of similar books. Notice how they make certain elements clear – what kind of story it is, what kind of readers might identify with the main character (and therefore enjoy the book) and what kind of action might take place.

It also helps to try to describe the book verbally to a friend.

But your synopsis should have prepared you. Once you've started thinking in summary form, you'll probably find usable versions pop into your head as you're making a cup of tea. Before you started the process of writing the synopsis it would have been impossible.

Cover letter

You need to introduce yourself and your novel.

1: Introduce your novel
Begin with a short paragraph explaining your novel's genre, how long it is and what your novel is about.

Following our email/telephone conversation I'm enclosing my novel Broken Glass.

Broken Glass is around 100,000 words long and is a thriller. It is the story of Jenny, whose new flatmate starts to take over her life. She muscles in on Jenny's friendships, borrows her clothes and steals from her bank account. When Jenny tries to get rid of her, she is dragged into a sinister world.

2 Introduce yourself
Next, explain who you are. Again keep it brief. This is like applying for a job – you explain just enough to show that you should be taken seriously for this particular role.

Don't include a CV. Don't list all the jobs you've done unless they are unusual and suggest you have a fund of experiences that will produce fascinating fiction. If you've had a lifelong career in banking or marketing, mention this so they know who you are, but move on to other more relevant information –

I'm 29 and my background is in marketing. Broken Glass is my first novel and was inspired by...

You don't have to say what your novel was inspired by, but it does add a nice personal touch.

If your novel is based on personal experiences that are unusual, mention that. But be aware of what is unusual. Most life events – divorces, bereavements, weddings, giving birth – happen to most people. Although they are landmarks they are not unusual. Being brought up in a children's home would be, though, as might joining the circus.

It will strengthen your case if you can say why you think this novel is timely and readers will be interested in its subject – for instance the credit crunch or exploring adventures in self-sufficiency.

Even better if you can find a statistic to back it up – eg a report that 40 per cent more people applied for allotments this year than last year. But only include these if you're sure they're accurate. (I just made that up, by the way, you'll need to find your own allotment statistic.) But be careful how you say these things. You want your choice of subject to look like personal passion, not a cynical marketing exercise.

If your novel is inspired by, or similar in concept to a successful one, you might want to say. Although some agents hate to see blockbusters name-checked for their own sake (*it's similar in tone to Twilight*), so be sparing with comparisons.

If you do use them, keep them short and to the point: *the novel plays with structure in a similar way to David Mitchell's Cloud Atlas* – but there's no need to go into more detail. Even if you could say some very perceptive things about *Cloud Atlas*, agents/publishers don't want an essay.

3: Other writing experience
If you've done creative writing courses it's worth mentioning, as it shows your dedication to your craft. If you've had professional help editing your manuscript, such as a report from a critiquing consultancy, this can help your manuscript to be taken more seriously.

Don't include a copy of the report, though. Even though it may list your strengths as a writer, the publisher wants to make up his or her own mind.

4: Language
Keep the letter factual but friendly. Don't use over-formal language – it's not a school essay.

Don't put anything self-deprecating or humble, such as *I hope my efforts might amuse or entertain, and won't irritate too much*. It's very annoying.

Don't try to be funny – it rarely works.

Don't tell them what kinds of books you like to read. Just keep to the point – who you are, what your novel's about and any reasons why you are the ideal person to write it.

Don't include a character listing. Agents and publishers don't like to be told what you intend them to think of the characters. They want to work this out for themselves.

And finally...

Print out your manuscript or manuscript excerpt according to the preferences of that particular publisher or agent. Or split it off into appropriate files, formatted according to their instructions. Pedantic, I know, but you want them in a good mood. Include an SAE if you want printed material back, or state in the letter that you're happy for them to recycle.

Include your letter. And your beautifully crafted synopsis.

Then, as my agent would say, propitiate the gods. Good luck.

Index

About the author

Roz Morris cut her authoring teeth by writing other people's novels. As a ghostwriter she has nearly a dozen titles in print, eight of them bestsellers. She is now coming out from under the ghosting sheet with novels of her own.

My Memories of a Future Life will be published in July 2011

She is also a freelance editor, and has guided many promising new writers to the stage where their work is taken seriously by agents and publishers.

When not wrestling her novels into shape or secretly scribbling for other authors, she can be found online at www.rozmorris.wordpress.com and on her blog www.nailyournovel.com, or explaining why her Twitter handle is @dirtywhitecandy. If you tweet too, do flit by and ask.